ON HUMAN SOVEREIGNTY

Sang Yun Han

BOSTON PRODIGY SCHOOL

ⓒ Boston Prodigy School
Author 저자/ Sang Yun Han 한상륜
Publisher 발행인/Boston Prodigy School 보스턴프라디지스쿨
  o CEO 대표/Young Hee Han 한영희
  o Address 주소/215-507, Gaepo-Ro 109 Gil 9, Gangnam-Gu,
            Seoul, Korea (06335)
            서울 강남구 개포로 109길 9, 215-507 (06335)
  o Registry No. 등록번호/2017-000043
  o Tel 전화/02-2226-0548
  o Web 홈페이지/http://www.bpskorea.org
  o Email 이메일/bpskorea@gmail.com
Printer 인쇄인/한국학술정보(주)
Issue Date 발행일/2018. 2. 3
ISBN 979-11-960882-1-7
Price 정가/₩15,000

TO MY WIFE

With Love, Respect, and Appreciation

TABLE OF CONTENTS

Preface..7
Chapter 1: Interpretation of Being..11
   I. The Result of Misinterpreting Meaning of Being............................12
   II. Critique of Misinterpretation of Being...14
   III. Meaning of Being...20
   IV. God as the Ground of Being..27
Chapter 2: Human Being...34
   I. Human as a Physical Being Named Body..36
   II. Human as a Spiritual Being..39
   III. Human as a Rational Being...42
   IV. Materialistic View on Human Being..47
Chapter 3: Reason..54
   I. Traditional Concept of Reason Before Kant....................................56
   II. German Idealism: Kant & Hegel..62
   III. Frankfurt School...66
   IV. Critique of Reason's Fundamentality in Contemporary Civilization
  71
Chapter 4: Morality...80
   I. The Essence of Morality...81
      (A) Unity of Knowledge and Conduct..82
      (B) Social Justice..86
      (C) Pursuit of Happiness..91
      (D) Divine Love..102
      (E) Existential Action..105
      (F) Categorical Imperative..110
   II. Relation of Reason and Morality...117
      (A) Schopenhauer's Critique of Kant's Categorical Imperative
     119
      (B) Critique Against Schopenhauer's Moral Philosophy
     130

  (C) Relation of Reason and Morality............137
Chapter 5: Society and Man............147
 I. Critique of Ideology............149
  (A) Concepts of Society............149
  (B) Critique of Main Ideology............152
  (C) Critique of Marx's Merchandise Value............157
   ① The Commodity as the Fundamental Unit of Capitalist Society............158
   ② The Relation between Use Value, Exchange Value, and Value............159
   ③ The Relation between Concrete and Abstract Labor............160
   ④ The Dialectical Contradictions in Marx's Identification in Treatment of the Commodity Form............162
   ⑤ The Culmination of Those Contradictions in the "Fetishism of Commodities"............166
   ⑥ Conclusion............169
 II. Human Sovereignty............170
  (A) Spiritual Life............172
  (B) Seeking for Truth............174
  (C) Economical Independence............175
  (D) Political Wisdom............177
  (E) Philanthropic Share............179
 III. New State as the Institution of Human Sovereignty............181
  (A) Freedom............181
  (B) Justice............183
  (C) Democracy............184
  (D) Social Welfare............185
  (E) Peace............186
ANNOTATIONS............189
BIBLIOGRAPHY............195

Preface

Man has innate tendency to include all objects, outward or inward, into his own mind territories as his belongings while concerning and fearing oneself in the evanescent world. From this self-centered propensity man seems to be incarcerated in his own deep-rooted prejudices and interests during his whole life, which has been inculcated by all kinds of outward influences like religion, philosophy, ideology, and all disciplines; even family origin, regional characteristics, ethnic or racial properties, and inevitable hereditary genes have worked as one's distorted mental pictures; furthermore wrong doctrines or information have been charged indiscriminately into one's own brain without the process of distilling false or wrong data, so that man's faculty of judging any situation has been defiled by all kinds of worldly futile values and hogwash. This terrible result has brought us havoc to be depraved into a hell of a world without any hope for the desirable society.

Man is by nature a political animal. If we deny this fact, it would endanger ourselves into being fallen into hands of wicked men who would damage our lives so seriously that we could not escape from their shackles. Man should act wisely in all political situation for his own well-being as well as others', but against all complicated mechanism of state life, we have only one means to correct wrong situation: ballot; maybe this is the unique tool for us to participate in the real politics and express our own wills, but after all, we would face the frustrated situation in which we have no other means but to burst into tears of resentment and drinking alcoholic beverages; then we must cast a ballot after painful consideration and resolute decision.

But despite our best ballot, all situations cannot be favorable to us, because choice between my profit and state well-being cannot be always corresponding. Man must escape from this contradictory situation to act politically wise or profitably, because the political deeds which are based on the wrong or false biases would result in the total destruction of all members in the society. In this purpose, this book shall try to criticize and escape from the past influential ontological thoughts of Being and Human Being, and from the past strong epistemological view of Reason, and from the past established concepts of Morality; afterward we shall go over to the relation of society and man with the critical purview of theory of society and man's position in the society, and this will follow the critique of present hegemonic ideologies like capitalism and communism, neo-liberalism and socialism with diagnosing presently processing tragedies of human history.

At this stage we will be able to figure out what guarantees human sovereignty which should be the ultimate goal of all political behaviors whether leaders or followers in the society. Although it will not be easily approved by many readers, human sovereignty should be interwoven into the highest standard of human dignity and absolute validity of human existence. Then, man must first establish the dignified relation of fellowship with God which is regarded as the creator, supervisor, protector, and judge of all life on this earth. This may seem religiously dogmatic, but if reviewing all high level of religion and most influential philosophies, some ultimate being in the universe has been believed to exist and be grasped vaguely in human cognizance, so that despite the epithet of the object, God has been supposed to exist and exert important power over us, then without the rightful fellowship with the God we cannot live our lives harmoniously and peacefully.

Second requisite is that we should secure the freedom from all lack of material condition, and this should be possible only by obtaining the social equality of opportunity to lead our livelihood by the state level, if not, the state would be almost deadly weapon to forfeit and oppress most members of the society; therefore without means of violence we must seek for the way of being guaranteed our material lives first of all, without which all other living conditions might be empty cant.

Third requisite is that we must have the socially equal opportunity of self-realization, and for this purpose we should not be checked or oppressed in any case if our living is legally justified; which means society has to guarantee all individuals to reach their self-realization; in any sense, the ultimate freedom from the interference or enforcement of the society must be presupposed for it. This signifies that society or state must concede that all individuals have each individuality, so that society or the state must not force individuals to follow their uniformity in the cause of total well-being of the society.

Fourth requisite is that all individuals should be equipped with the highest level faculty of judgement to choose their leaders, civil servants, or public officials; for this task all individuals should realize how much important their individual ballots should be, thereby individuals should think much of their own rights despite its divided triviality of their ballots; then they should study escaping from all political unreasonableness or ideological dogmas by sharpening their power of reasoning from being informed all correct and good information and cultural refinement.

    Tragically human history eloquently shows the heinous dialectics of hegemony and bondage, and the ruled has been overly maltreated from the rulers whether monarchs, democratic leaders, or communist regimes, so in any sense man has been the inevitable poor creatures to be oppressed, tortured, threatened, and forfeited by the public power of the state; then here we must visualize the ideal state in which all individuals will have been guaranteed their material lives as well as spiritual life for their perfect self-realization. In this purport, this book will deal with the ideal new state although it is somewhat short of the perfect picture of best society.

Chapter 1: Interpretation of Being

Since launching on speculation of Being from the beginning of human existence on this earth, man has been searching for all kinds of way to explain what is Being and what makes this Being and how it can be functioned and processed. Someone searched for the principle of operation of the sky and stars, earth and mountains and seas, trees and woods, animals and insects. In short, they tried to find the principle of the operation of the universe, and after long effort, puts forward the one ultimate being by which all other things can be explained. Thales designated it 'water', Plato 'fire, earth, air, and water', Pythagoras 'number', and in India, 'Brahman', and in China, Laozi 'Tao', Confucius 'Tian', Buddha, 'Dharma' .

With time passage on so-called philosophers established their own system of explanation of Being and with confident satisfaction they dared to say that they had already completed their philosophy and encouraged people to follow their dogmas and devoted themselves to their own system. In any sense, history of mankind has been the battle fields of their thinking results because all established ideologies have forced people to stand by their own camps, if not, more often than not, merciless massacre followed immediately.

In this purport, we will discuss meaning of Being, firstly from the terrible present results coming from traditional interpretation of Being, secondly we will criticize their false interpretation of Being, and finally we will reveal our thinking about Being in the totally different perspectives against traditional concepts of Being.

I. The Result of Misinterpreting Meaning of Being

In human history, ancient times seemed to be showcase of peoples' mythical symbolic interpretation which had explained the phenomena of the world by unknown mysterious beings like spirits, demons, and elf, but this mysterious superstition has been replaced by the more complex and elaborate dogmas in the name of religion. From the result religious power has exerted more profound influence on human lives than any idea on men; of course after the initiators, their successors have enriched the contents, have complicated system of the religion more elaborately, and demarcated themselves from other religious boundaries and have been extending limitlessly.

But almost tens of thousand years was too long time to grasp human mind continually and persuade them to support their doctrines faithfully, and in the midst of violent struggles in the camps of orthodoxies and dissenters, very brave men appeared on the human history with very reasonable but experimental ideology of fighting against seemingly wealthy but greedy men in the cause of human equality, incensing people to raise arms in hands to forfeit their properties and distribute them to the people equally; their slogan was so attractive in the view of poor people without any will and power, but they could not initiate the rebel for themselves against the wealthy and rulers, so instead of them a few intellectuals who had warm, open, but sometime ambitious mind to their neighbor's hardships organized their sympathizers and defied the ruling classes with fortified vested rights. They established their own utopian kingdoms and tried to equalize all persons regardless of their inherent talents or hot wishes to be wealthy, even killing tens of millions of dissenters for their slogan, 'From each according to his ability, to each according to his needs'[1]. If this miraculous but contradictory slogan could have been fulfilled, perhaps human history might have gone toward the unexpected way, but it proved a mirage of the oasis in the sands because of its inherent contradiction.

Human history starting from the myth and superstition had turned to the dogmas of religions, but before just two centuries human jerked its direction from gods to science, and from the results, politics and economics also have been sharply changed to satisfy the ideology of the era only to bring about the most terrible world on human history, which might endanger all human beings on this earth, and we are now facing the heinous era of imminent war of imperialism versus terrorism; in fact we are now watching the eschatological symptoms of degeneration and collapse of human kind.

Here, we must retrospect all important thoughts coming from myth, religion, philosophy, and ideologies which have influenced human kind this or that way, but this task should be made with the heart of only loving truth and the keen eyes of criticism against all kinds of prejudices, favoritism, partisanism, and falsehood, with which this task should be another hogwash to lead astray readers into another dogma, and just add up another wicked suggestion to make human beings into depravity and destruction. But we must limit the range of the texts and real reflection on human lives in the past and present, which are still prevalent in our world with substantial effect on our way of thinking, living standards, and the ruling system.

II. Critique of Misinterpretation of Being

Essentially, all theories and suggestion about the meaning of Being have their own merits and some portion of truth, but that does not guarantee their validity; of course this critique also has some merits and portion of truth, but this also can be based on a kind of misinterpretation of Being. In other word, all human thoughts cannot brag that their own system can be the only and ultimate truth, but should be humble in thinking that we are in the process of grasping the true meaning of Being with our best effort, and although this cannot be justified at this time and shows some lack of truth, maybe our descendants would try to add better theory and advanced thinking system, so that we should be satisfied with just suggesting another interpretation of Being. In short, there has been no absolute truth in any human interpretation of Being, so we must not be deceived by any false theories and suggestions whether or not they are beneficial to us in the name of practicality. If we are declined to some myth, religion or ideology, we surely feel inclined to espouse it vehemently without any process of proof, so from this tendency we come to

Chapter 1: Interpretation of Being 15

be labeled some supporters of myth, religion, or ideology; therefore first of all we must desert all kinds of prejudices and bad tendency for or against some specific idea; if not, our efforts would endanger us into trap or pit of falsehood and deception.

What is Being?

In his book *Being and Time*, Heidegger argues that in order to interpret Being we must first interpret Being-with, the characteristics of Human Being, because he can be the pathway to enter interpreting Being, and for this purpose we must first analyze our present existential circumstances. But after all interpretation he concludes that Time is the original characteristics of Being, for we are now in all the aspects of Time. His idea is no more than the same interpretation of Buddhism which suggests that all things and phenomena are ruled in the time category, of which characteristics is but evanescence.

In other word, everything is being ruled by the time frame of change and disappearance, so seeming phenomena is another expression of naught; therefore we don't need to obsess over the evanescent beings, and should empty ourselves and be freed from Dharma which has been stored up to us from the moment of our birth, and this is the only way of evading pain from birth, agedness, sickness, and death. Here we can know that Heidegger and Buddhism interpreted the meaning of Being in the perspectives of time category, but this interpretation overlooked most important thing beyond the true aspect of physical disappearance of our beings.

One of the famous Korean Confucian thinkers in 15th century, Gyungduk Seo suggested that all things remain after physical disappearance in the form of Chi, illustrating that the fire of candle disappears but the Chi in the fire is transformed into another form in the universe, so every being can remain everlastingly in the form of Chi; therefore the Chi in human being can be transformed into another form named Ghost, and he warned materialists of the danger of overlooking the existence of Chi and its transformation Ghost.

The Confucianism has thought that the principle of operating universe is physical one, so in the mutual operation of all beings, human beings are also deeply interrelated to the operation, so that human lives are ethically expressed in the phenomena of the physical beings and its operational principle, Chi and Li.

The Taoism initiator Laozi thought that the ultimate principle of operation of the universe is 'Tao', which cannot be expressed in language or any symbol, because it is too vast and propound to be grasped in human cognizance. They emphasized the undoing and naturalness for human well being and leaving natural world alone.

In human history the important achievement of Indian Hinduism is that they looked into the reality of the universe and expressed it as Brahman, and when the great Brahman of the universe are revealed in human beings, it is expressed as small Brahman, and when they are corresponded wholly, true unity comes true. But from their explanation of Being in all kinds of deity by the adamant hierarchy, we cannot get any

Chapter 1: Interpretation of Being

meaningful interpretation of Being.

But in contrast to oriental thinkers, ancient Greek philosophers interpreted Being in the perspectives of materialism or spiritualism. In materialists Being is only grasped in the eyes of observation and experiments, and in the analysis of material world, we can come close to the real Being, which tendency was expressed as the ultimate principle of the universe (in fact, the earth and solar system) by some elements like water, fire, air, wind, and atom, etc, but these hypotheses seem very unreasonable and prejudiced in the eyes of spiritualism; therefore spiritualist suggested gods as the original essence of Being, and endowed them with all kinds of unsearchable myth for explanation of this world; of course its fantastic interpretation of Being did not satisfy all intelligent thinkers; nevertheless their symbolic system of gods has influenced human beings so profoundly that whether we believe it or not, ancient Greek mythology echoes through this age in the system of symbol, sign, and psychology; therefore whether or not we interpret meaning of Being in any direction, we cannot evade from mythology and psychology, because our interpretation of Being has been inevitably immersed in their thoughts. In this sense human kind has not yet evaded from the illusion of myth and false doctrines; rather in the midst of inhumane chaos of political and economical ideology, it has been strengthened more drastically in the cause of god and destructed humanity by the flagrant terror.

Western Middle Ages has been called dark ages because of the oppression by the ruling hegemony of Catholic Christianity, whose thinkers tried to interpret Being in the perspectives of God, the creator of heaven and earth and all beings in the universe. They were supposed to have the strong weapon named Holy Scriptures, but they could not take advantage of it because it could not persuade intellectuals and unbelievers when they thought it was a kind of myth and Israel history. Furthermore, they had to be influenced from the Greek philosophical system in the explanation of Being, which must be explained in the Christian doctrines; in other word, God could be only responsible agent for expounding Being; therefore their explanation had to be mixed with scriptural accounts as well as Greek philosophy and clumsy scientific facts which had budded in the Arabic world.

After collapse of Papacy the humanist thinkers argued that human mind had been freed from the bondage of myth and illusion, and man should focus on the scientific truth for the development of human well-being. This thinking led almost intelligent people to try to grasp the meaning of Being in the science, and from the result theology was reduced to a very small practical discipline to train future ministers, and in the position of theology, philosophy and science were seated proudly and proclaimed that they would guarantee prosperity and advancement of humankind. In their vehement effort, science started to reveal the secrets of Being in material region, and a lot of shocking facts overthrew the old regimes of divinity and fundamentally changed human thoughts regarding the meaning of Being. They argued that there had been no God or gods and spiritual beings and there would be no future

Chapter 1: Interpretation of Being

world after our death. This agenda has been established so strongly with ample evidences in the form of scientific findings and the certain results from scientific observations and experiments. Their astounding achievements of scientific investigation could lay seemingly sure way of human prosperity, so that in modern times most philosophers proclaimed confidently that they were materialists.

In keeping abreast of the scientific development, philosophy also turned around its speculation not on the essential being but on the epistemological method; that is, they had to focus on finding the method to find the criterion of truth, and they divided their searching way into two camps: empiricism and rationalism. They fought against each other terribly, so that one party could not concede another one; empiricism proposed experience as the only possible way of reaching truth, but rationalism put forward reason for it. But Kant synthesized their bloody results in simple way of criticizing both weaknesses and merging advantages; his long painstaking feats of speculation resulted in the fundamental tragedies of human reason, that is, established tendency of material human being.

Being has lost its fair share in human thinking history although in contemporary times German philosopher Heidegger showed some substantial possibility of interpreting Being in the direction of human being as Being-with as I said in the beginning of this section. But it should not be such trivial theme as has been neglected or hidden in the human history of speculation; rather it should be clarified above all, because without it all established systems of humankind could be endangered all the more with the time passage on. The reason is very clear; interpretation of Being must be the cornerstone on which all true and healthy society should be built.

III. Meaning of Being

What is Being? Is Being material or spiritual or some other reality?

As regards to these questions we must first clarify the essence of Being. In other word, Being cannot be limited in scientific method, because it cannot be grasped by it, and Being is not easily expressed in language, because already it transcends our cognizance. Briefly speaking, Being is 'Essence of Something' revealed to us outwardly in the form of material existence; this is summarized as 'Revelation of Something', and this includes some code which we cannot decode easily, but as we see in the circumstances of our everyday living, we can look into the purpose of some furniture, utensils, machines, and tools; for example, a seat is used for purpose of seating, and television is used for watching some news or information or entertainment; then all natural beings have their own purposes; then we can vaguely interpret that all outward natural items have their own purposes. This is not general meaning of Being in the natural world, because in contrast to Hegel's argumentation, natural Being in the world is not such as the revealed reason of the Absolute.

Chapter 1: Interpretation of Being

Aristotle conceived this characteristic of the material being as 'soul' by illustrating that wax has the soul of 'melting'; axe has the soul of 'cutting'; the eyes have 'the sight' as the soul. In this purport, Aristotle is the forerunner in the materialistic view of the soul in his thinking that every item, material or immaterial, has the soul as the animator of that item. If we extend his thinking to modern items like automobile, its soul is 'automatic moving', so if a car is out of order, and if it doesn't move, the soul disappears. He applies the corresponding principle of the soul to human, and the human soul is no other than animator of our body; therefore if our body dies, our soul disappears immediately, and all set with no existence.

Some years ago physicist Steven Hawking said in an interview of UK *Guardian*, "I regard the brain as a computer which will stop working when its components fail. There is no heaven or afterlife for broken down computers; that is a fairy story for people afraid of the dark."

His saying is that human is a kind of exquisite computer, which loses its function when out of order. This is a contemporary trend regarding the soul or mind. Against this materialistic view of soul, Plato, Augustine, Aquinas, and Descartes held the immaterialistic view of soul; after them, in contrast to general view, Kant also held materialistic view on the soul, and after him the main stream of western philosophy has flowed to the materialistic view of the soul; then Aristotle's idea of Being as soul cannot be justified by us, because the essence of Being cannot be grasped in the materialistic view at all although outward objects can reveal some code of Being, the essence of Being is not just material; rather we can parenthesize it something unknown, which can be paralleled by Kant's Ding an sich, but here we should not dare to conceive it as material or immaterial, because still it exists before us as an existential reality. One point which we can be impressed upon by this thinking is that Being surely exists as essence of something, and we can just see its outward phenomena in the spatio-temporal variability.

The second meaning of Being is 'Relativity'. But this concept is not the same as Einstein's Theory of Relativity in which physical being should be influenced in their form of time and space by the influence of gravity field when light passes through it. In the universe all things have their own uniqueness in their relationship with others, so in any sense Being is expressed in the relation of all things, but it doesn't mean it doesn't have its own individuality. In any sense individuality seems to be the essential part of Being, but in other sense, individual is lying in the context of relational mutuality; therefore all things show all different properties inherently from the birth, but have existed together with others unconditionally, so that all beings should be mutually influenced on each other, and all things including human beings should be interpreted as coexistent beings regardless of their own difference and uniqueness. This shall be extended to the sociality of human kind as the social animal.

Even if one important meaning of Being is 'Relativity', the true meaning of relativity is not limited in existential tenure of life on this earth, because always it extends itself to

Chapter 1: Interpretation of Being   23

self-centered ego however it may be divisive and differentiated to the unlimited level. Here we can conceive the third meaning of Being is 'Self', without which things cannot exist at all; therefore all things should focus on sustaining themselves in any milieu, which we call egoism. But there is no denying the fact that egoism has been the main dynamic power of Being, so that all things in the universe have centered on living on this planet, not walking on the illusionary oases of paradise without any real activities, but during those times almost every thoughts have focused on unreal fantasy, by which temporal satisfaction has been guaranteed but it passed too speedily to stay permanently; rather sometimes it hurt people in this or that way; finally its charlatan cure was disclosed as a deception, never functioning any more as the opiate of the general people. If some doctrines, whether religion or ideology or philosophy, negates this egoism of Being, it would surely malfunction in the complicated struggles of real life.

The fourth meaning of Being is 'Infinite', which includes infinity and infinitesimal; in other word, Being is limitless, so all the trial to find the extreme end in the largeness or smallness has been useless and may be impossible to finish the last stage, because the substantiality of Being is no finality. Although modern science has shown off its brilliant achievements in the Quantum Mechanics and Big Bang theory, the former has been blocked off in the present stage, because their suggestions have not been proved experimentally, and just showed imaginary idea of intelligent physicists. But even if we divide matter indefinitely searching for the final particle, there would be no definite such one, and the so-called Top Particle is also another imaginary one which quantum mechanics physicist named arbitrarily, and after that there should be another particle and more and more.......

Big Bang theory seems also a hypothesis which validity cannot be gotten through all kinds of experiments and observations of astronomy and physics, for this seemingly epoch-making theory is no more than an imaginary hypothesis resulted from the brain of bizarre scientist whose narrow and prejudiced thinking and idea made people astounded at his shockingly fresh idea that this universe has been born accidentally from a pin of a hole, and boundlessly extended to the infinite, has the 11 dimension, and present all beings in the universe is the products of pure contingency. How much brilliant and marvelous but groundless hypothesis!

Scientists have jeered at philosopher's thinking for the reason that it looks like a fiction without any scientific base, but once reaching the top level, scientist must use imaginary faculty, because without it they cannot build up their foundation of scientific theory, and after proclaiming their theory, they need not prove the validity, because it is almost impossible to prove their idea; rather theirs are also discourses about Being without any proof, so scientists as well as philosophers should not brag that their idea is final one and any new idea shall not be necessary for expounding Being.

The fifth meaning of Being is 'Naught", from which the One comes out and from the One everything in the universe originates. This Naught is the essential characteristics of Being,

Chapter 1: Interpretation of Being   25

and Being comes out from it and returns to it. In Confucianism and Taoism, this is called 'Apolarity', from which Taiji comes out, and this is also divided into Yin-Yang, and this brings forth Four Figures and Eight Trigrams and Sixty Four Symptoms. Through these physical doctrines, they tried to explain principle of the universe (in fact the world of Earth) and human lives, and tell fortunes. But this idea of Naught originated from ancient Korean thinkers more than 5,000 years ago, and it explained the physical operation of the Heaven, Earth, and Human; that is, Naught equals Apolarity, which brings forth the One, and it bears Big Three: Heaven, Earth, and Human, and Five Elements: water, tree, fire, earth, and metal, but the One is divided into Yin-Yang, and Big Three is divided into Yang-Heaven (day), Yin-Heaven (night), Yang-Earth (earth), Yin-Earth (underground), Yang-Human (male), Yin-Human (female), from this result numbers of operation of this world comes out. The operation number of heaven is seven, the one of the earth is eight, and the one of human is nine, but these all are operated in the One, so that the completion number is ten.

The origin of oriental philosophy is supposed to come from this principle, so that in the orient, philosophy, number, medicine, music, martial arts, and social system have been based on this doctrine which has been called 'Divine Authorized Scripture', and even our Korean alphabet was made by taking advantage of this principle. Nowadays this philosophy is called 'Three-One Philosophy' in Korea.

Here we do not want to ramble on the oriental philosophy

uselessly, but for explaining meaning of Being we just need to explain the meaning of Naught. This concept appears in the Genealogy of the Old Testament as chaos.

The sixth meaning of Being is 'Eternity'. This means that Being shall not disappear or be abolished, because its own identity is self-revelation; in other word, Being exists permanently regardless of its various forms and functions. Being is always itself, it does not deceive itself, and it does not hide itself as other, because Being everlastingly reveals itself in some physical form, but after the demise of its physical form, it continues its identity. Although all kinds of things come and stay in this world for temporal time and ceaselessly transforms themselves and withers and demises, their original status in the universe shall not disappear because of its eternity of Being. This idea is radically different from Nietzsche's eternal recurrence, because he borrowed the concept from doctrine of samsara in Hinduism. This idea says that all beings in the universe are recurring in various forms, so that birth and death are not different but same phenomenon.

To this stage, we have reviewed meaning of Being from criticizing important doctrines of myth, religion, and philosophy to establishing our own theories, so that now we have come to seize some outlines of true meaning of Being although it is not perfect and satisfying all. But in order to clarify Being more fundamentally, we must delve the first principle of Being through which all its other meanings are unified into this, and for which human beings have struggled sharply but to this date it has not been satisfying to all intellectuals, and from which all

Chapter 1: Interpretation of Being   27

false and unverified hypotheses have been brought up to the stage of history, but by which all tragedies of humankind have been worsened and worsened to the level of heinous terrorism of contemporary days; then the ultimate meaning of Being should come from the concept of the God, so from next section we are going to review the concept of God without any religious or doctrinal bias.

IV. God as the Ground of Being

What is God and what is it related to Being and how can we interpret God unprejudicedly? As to these questions we should desert all hardened attitude against the concept as if we were to treat religious one, especially Christian one, and should look into it with the sanest mind, because the truth can be obtained to the most inquisitive but generous heart with impartiality; therefore we must agree that God is not religious concept or idea; rather it is the most clear concept to denote the first principle of Being, so that we need not worry about its being dogmatic character from the religious or maniac emotion.

What is God? Does God exist? Is it different from gods? As regards to these questions, we are going to answer one by one. First of all, God is transcendental concept which excels all kinds of visible or invisible Being despite our all researches; therefore God is beyond Being as the originator and animator of Being, and this idea looks like the Christian concept that God is the creator of Heaven, Earth, Man and all things in the universe, and supervisor as well as intercessor of human beings. In Christianity God is expressed as the humane God with personality who formed Israel, leading, punishing, even saving Israelites in human history. Aristotle's concept of God is the first principle of Being by which all Being is possible, so his idea of God is the unmoved mover of the world. But his idea of God seems very materialistic view based on the physical substance. Spinoza's concept of God is no more than a pantheism about the natural world, because he looked upon all beings in the universe as revealed God. Hegelian thinking about the Absolute is as well the paraphrase of Christian concept of God in view of ideal Reason, but his idea runs toward mixing physical beings with spiritual being in the name of reason, so that he pointed at the side of God's material characteristics in the development of human history on this earth.

Here we must go back to the first question, 'What is God?' Firstly, I said that God is beyond Being as the originator and animator of Being, but I want to go further philosophically about the concept of God, because without establishing concept of God correctly, we cannot expect human enhancement any longer, so this is a really striking theme to have to investigate but there is no other theme harder than this one that we neglect recklessly for the reason of anti-religion or anti-Christianity. If Being originated from God and it has been animated by God, then are there more concepts about God? Here I must say that Being must return to God although its physical being disappears, then in this sense God is always with Being as the owner, so that all things should be oriented toward God despite its being invisibility.

To this stage, we discussed about the identity of God as the originator, animator, and owner of Being, but here we must say that God is over Being as the supervisor of Being, watching us all in any way, because if Being is originated, animated, and owned by God, already Being is going through in the process of God, and this is expressed in the universal rule, so that the deviated Being from the ordinary course of God, shall be dealt with this or that way, and this is defined as judgment.

From now on we shall need to discuss God's essential property in response to previous question, 'What is God?'. Firstly we must not think that God is material being with physical substance, but if it were true, God cannot be beyond Being, because material Being should be included in this natural world and be subjected to the rule of gravitation, but God excels all material beings, so that it is impossible for God to be physical being like humans; then is God spiritual being like angel or demon? No, God cannot be spiritual, for spiritual being cannot act in the material world, because it has no substantial form expressed outwardly; then we must think God's essential property in other ways; rather God is not defined as material or spiritual being, for such dualism is a kind of human way of dividing some categories into two convenient divisive way of classification; then God cannot be classified into any categories of material or spiritual being. Looking into the essential property of God deeply, God seems not defined material or spiritual; rather it is transcendental and comprehensive.

Concerning the question, 'Does God exist?', we are inclined to accept its existence, because whether we admit or negate it, there must be something beyond Being; in other word, Being can be justified only under the provision of some fundamental and transcendental Being whether we define it God or the Absolute or the First Principle or the Mover or something, without which we can never cognize phenomenal world or Ding an sich; if easily explaining, we continually live in the consecutive consciousness and in it we have included some outer or inner phenomena without knowing the correct reality, but in the most complicated speculation we can encode some secrets of physical world around us as well as our existential circumstances of everyday living. But if there is no underlying code, all physical world as well as mind field should be no more than messy chaos without order or rule; then we must posit some unknown Being beyond, with, and over us, whether we label it materially or spiritually or comprehensively.

Though conceding that there is no personifying God in the universe, we can vaguely guess that this universe has been operated by some mysterious system, and if we designate it materially instead of God, the materialistic reality of the universe shall be such Being as God; then we are now considering the material reality is the ultimate Being of operating all beings. In other word, they strongly argue that there is no such Being as God, but after all, they presuppose unconsciously the nature as God although they do not openly say God; easily speaking, to atheists, natural world is God however emphatically they insist that there be no God and all phenomena and essence of this world is no other than the material operation of the universe, so in some sense, materialists are not atheists although they surely negate the fact, because they believe in natural world as God. But atheists are also not atheists in that they do believe that there is no God; in fact they believe in no God, and to them no God is God.

As to the question, "Is God different from gods?" I will say, yes, God is clearly different from gods, because in human history all kinds of gods appeared and disappeared according to their fascinated power to men and women, and to this date we humans have more than several hundreds of thousands of gods in our everyday living, inwardly or outwardly to our mind, so however much we denied the existence of gods, they have lived together with us, and already have become part of our lives. The scholars of religion have suggested that we have had them because of inevitable fear of unknown world or human avarice to live luxuriously by taking advantage of absolute beings in the universe, so that gods have been the objects of human personality with the same property and characteristics as human beings-love, jealousy, greed, sexual desire, hatred, animosity, generosity, anger, fury, violence, intrigue, slyness, and wish, but in contrast to man, they have eternal life; that is, man is mortal, and gods are immortal. From Greek and Roman myths to oriental Hinduism, Buddhism, shamanism and even today's Voodoo of African originality, all gods are humane and are regarded as human reflection of some wish; this is so tragic to human destiny, because in spite of limitless number of gods in the human world, we have not only been damaged by gods but also have been fatally endangered by gods in the terrible destructive properties from such dangerous gods.

God is not limited in any categories of human cognizance, because essentially it excels Being although it has been always with us, so that God cannot be grasped by our human faculty except divine spirit which has been supposed to be endowed us with by him and cannot be found in any scientific method and research; only the very limited number of what we call saints have guessed vaguely in the intuitively profound inspiration, so they have called him by this or that connotation, but gods have been products of human imagination and needs from which all bizarre acts have been resulted for their own profits; some gods have seemed to have ontological ground because of its complicity with ruling classes for their metaphysical doctrines and magnificent worship rituals; even they have been called high religion, but other gods have been fabricated from crude idea and foolish thinking, so that they look to be ludicrous and groundless; for example, in ancient Egypt, there had been god of fly, and god of frog; in Thailand cat is worshipped as god; in Hinduism bull and cow are regarded as incarnation of gods; furthermore in Japan it is reported that more than eighty thousand gods have existed.

Although there have been some profitable influence to us by these low worship forms, there have been always conflicts and fighting against each other among human groups and from the flagrant fighting for hegemony, almost all religions have brought in havoc to humankind to the degree that healing and restoration would not be possible at all from the futile illusion and darkness of idolatry; rather we can suppose that these may well be called good examples of how much foolish and dull may human mind be! In this purport, we don't need to concede any god for the benefit of humankind, but God should be kept for the enhancement of human society as the only foundation to guarantee well being and true prosperity of human beings, for as I have said to this stage that God exists self-evidently, has revealed himself in the process of nature and in our heart, and has even intervened in the affairs of humankind this or that way, so that if we deny the existence of God, we would lose the true base of our civilization and would fall to the deformed monsters or inhumane machines struggling for the economical profits or scientific ostentation.

In the human history of philosophy all trial and efforts to prove existence of God have failed because they tried to prove it in the perspectives of religion or materialism or deism, but it is basically impossible, because they could not explain God and persuade people to be confident of the existence of God, so that in my short explanation, I don't think that I can also convince people of its validity, but we must bear in mind that God should be philosophically interpreted continually for laying the most desirable cornerstone of social reformation. In summary, I consistently assert that God exists, be connected to us very closely, and should be the cornerstone of our civilization for the reformation of our society.

Chapter 2: Human Being

The question, 'What is man?' has been one of the most controversial theme in the history of mankind, because all the disciplines have asked for their own shares, suggesting their own thoughts on this topic; therefore all kinds of explanation and theory have appeared on the stage of competition venue of human thoughts. As the representative idea of theirs we have had, 'Man is a rational animal.', 'Man is a social animal.' from Aristotle, and from Cassirer, "Man is a symbolic animal."[2], but despite these marvelous definitions of man, we have had not finite definition of man; rather we shall have the more difficulty, the more we pursue the truth about human being, because as we see, all philosophical suggestions since Socrates in occidental world have been nothing more than the doctrine of man, so we have had huge pile up of books and dissertations on this theme, but still we need more urgently establish genuine human theory for the desirable reformation of society than ever, without which we shall not do anything for it and with which we can only lay the firm foundation of our good society.

But here we should not bend toward our profitable interpretation of human being however much it would benefit us, for we are not the only creatures in the world, and we only do not have absolute rights to exist on the Earth; then we should pay attention to unbiased and harmonious truth of man; furthermore we should not set up easily human theory from the specific perspective of man, because like the concept of Being, human being is so much complicated and transcendental one beyond our cognizance, so that in any sense we can say that man is a dialectically metaphysical animal with body.

But as to the interpretation of human body, a physical being, we have not had standard agreement to it, since human body itself is a metaphysical one with something mysterious and insolvable; however, that cannot be the excuse to skip explanation of human body. Nevertheless, we must focus on philosophical interpretation of human body, not on its anatomical or biological characteristics. Here we are going to expound some better interpretation of human body inherited from ancient times of oriental world, which was believed to have brought forth oriental foundation of metaphysical thought, medicine, and martial arts.

I. Human as a Physical Being named Body

There is no denying that we humans have each body which is surely physical and is ruled under the law of gravitation and the natural world, so however much repeatedly we try to evade from the material condition we cannot evade it; at last we will see our own pathetic sight in which we suffer from all kinds of stress, disappointment, and frustration, so that we cannot neglect or deny the importance of human body as the base of our living on this planet.

Of course, human body has been known anatomically to some degree by the great advancement of medical appliances, and from the superb instruments we sometimes have much optimism that we can analyze and research any part of human body; even with that medical excellence we can get over most of human diseases, but this is very arrogant and foolish thinking of human body, which would not pave the triumphant victory over even a small virus of cold. In some sense western medicine has been developed into analyzing, finding, dissecting, and operating human body, but it has not penetrated into the fundamental world of human body; therefore their curing method has been called allopathic.

But profound insights of oriental thinkers found human body not on the separate physical world or isolated physical being; rather they thought that human body is the reflection of the universe, so its universal principle is included in the human body. In Genesis 1: 27 of Old Testament, it is written, "So God created man in his own image, in the image of God he created them; male and female he created them."[3] Here we cannot know what the image of God is, some said it is human reason, others morality, but in Mormonism they have suggested the anthropomorphism, that is, man looks like God in his figure, while oriental thinkers thought that in human body the principle of the universe is perfectly included. Although as to the human being oriental thinking focuses on physical aspects of man, occidental idea has looked upon human body as body including soul or body operating materially.

Korean ancient Three-One philosophy revealed that human being consists of three essences: Nature (power of knowledge), Life (power of livelihood), Sex (power of reproduction), and these three essences consist of three substances: Mind (medium of knowledge), Chi (medium of livelihood), Body (medium of reproduction), and these three substances results in three realities: Feeling (way of knowledge), Breath (way of livelihood), Touch (way of reproduction). These three realities are transformed into eighteen boundaries; from Feeling there come joy, fear, sorrow, anger, greed, and hatred; from Breath, fragrance, stench, chill, fever, dryness, and dampness; from Touch, sound, color, odor, taste, lust, and touch.

The ancient Korean philosophers think that human being is an incarnation of three-one principle which has generated Heaven, Earth, and Man; therefore in human body five elements of water, tree, fire, earth, and metal are harmoniously operated; they are represented by kidney (Yin water), liver (Yin tree), heart (Yin fire), spleen (Yin earth), lung (Yin metal), and these organs have also each Yang counterpart; bladder (Yang water), gall bladder (Yang tree), small intestine (Yang fire), stomach (Yang earth), colon (Yang metal).

In oriental thinking, mind is the reflection of the unified function of all organs in the body, so in oriental thinking there has been no dualism like western tendency of body and mind, which has resulted in all kinds of argumentation and struggles against each other, even they brought about fundamental difference of political ideology in theism (capitalism) and materialism (communism). Despite their antipodal tendency, both camps have equally fought for the possession rights of material beings, so nowadays speaking about spiritual being means anachronistic thought and moron's stupidity in both ranks. Then, they should agree to my interpretation of mind from the oriental perspectives of body and mind unification; in other word, no body, no mind. This looks so simple if agreed upon by all intelligent persons of the world, but the matter is not such a simple one as most of world people reach the agreement, because it is the final verdict standing by the materialist's camps if we consistently argue that body and mind is one.

Traditional philosophy has tried to squeeze all possible explanation that mind is the reflection of physical body and at last mind is just nothing more than material being, so that we can make artificial intelligence if we can analyze the complex mechanism of our brain by the great help of best computer system and all advanced disciplines of biological sciences; the result is the boom of artificial intelligence in all fields of industry: robot, cell phone, computer, semi-conductor, car, and engineering; maybe in near future some grotesque monster like Das Vader in the movie of Star Wars might appear on the unified Earth Empire as the commander-in-chief by the help of brilliant art intelligence.

Here I am going to turn around from this simply materialistic view of body and mind to totally new interpretation of body as the holder of life originality-spirit, soul, and form. This interpretation might be the bizarre and unfamiliar to western philosophers if we posit spirit as the pristine vitality to make all human soul function intelligently or foolishly or depravedly in the human body, and from the results the original human soul, there arise specific form of man, and shall be transformed into any kind of deformity changed from the brilliance of divine character and original purity. In this sense we must say human being is spiritual, but this is not religious interpretation from biblical foundation so as to force people to have faith in God; rather we should look into the true reality of the universe, which cannot be defined as just the material being although it has been processed materially in our eyes; therefore we must look into the hidden mystery of the world in the penetrating eyesight of intelligence beyond the futile dualism of matter and mind or body or soul, because in spite of our negation the universe was, is, and will be in the astonishing wonder of birth, growth, and death in every fields of life.

II. Human as a Spiritual Being

What is spirit? Is the so-called divine animator of human body as well as soul? Is it just material vitality endowed with man at birth, which makes man human being? Is spirit different from soul? What is its relation to human soul and form?

Answering these questions might be very dangerous to answer, for it shall be widely open to the attack from the materialists and atheists because they have thought that essentially whole phenomena and their function of this world come from the materialistic universe which is conceived as an organic nature. Even religious people have denied the existence of human spirit although they have believed in some absolute being in the universe. Perhaps ancient people who have been regarded as primitive once strongly believed that all things in the world have their own spirits, so all phenomena in the world and human fortunes and misfortunes, even omens good or bad were believed to come from the invisible spirits, so that they worshipped natural things with unknown awe or fear; sometimes they were frightened by thunder and lightning; they felt great terror from huge ferocious animals like tiger, bear, or huge reptiles; they were marveled at the enormous tree or mountains; all giant or solemn things in the universe were the important objects of worship; they even bowed down before the Sun, Moon, and the Stars; they believed that all things in the universe were the divine revelation, so in the serious drought and flood, they attributed all responsibility to the leader's evils, even killing them to appease gods' fury. These ideas are called animism.

In my thinking, the Christian approach to spirit seems very reasonable, because they thought God breathed his

Chapter 2: Human Being

breath to man's nostrils and they became animate beings; this fact is seen in Genesis 2: 7 of Old Testament.

> "the LORD God formed the man from the dust of the ground and breathed into his nostrils the breath of life, and the man became a living being."4)

Here the breath of life (Hebrew: נִשְׁמַת חַיִּים Nisimat Haim) is another expression of Hebrew 'רוּחַ" ruha', Greek 'πνευμα pneuma', and English 'spirit', and this connotes 'wind', 'breath', 'life', and from this word, we can know that spirit is a kind of the essential power that makes man alive. Here we should distinguish it from the soul, mind, or reason.

In oriental philosophy, spirit connotes medium between this world and that world; this means that life and death are interacted in each other's region, so that life and death cannot be different from each other; rather we must realize that there is no special boundary of life and death, because life itself is another side of death, and death is also another side of life. Anyway spirit should be understood irrespective of dualism of body and soul, and it is the unifying essence which can make man human being.

As to the question, 'Is spirit different from soul?', I will say yes, because if spirit is understood as the essence of human being which makes man alive, then we can think that it is no more than animator of man, but soul has been understood differently from spirit and had been conceived as the faculty of mind, reason, and consciousness, then spirit should be understood as the holder of soul, and from soul human mind can be possible; in other word, soul is the receptacle of mind, reason, and consciousness. Of course here we should have the necessity to demarcate these three concepts, but since the age of reason (17 century) almost all epistemological suggestions have equaled soul, mind, reason, and even consciousness, and from their undifferentiated mixture of theories all kinds of chaotic argumentation have arisen to make inquisitive people confused about the possibility of human knowledge; these also brought in terrible tragedies in the division of two camps: theism and materialism.

III. Human as a Rational Being

Here we need to discuss some more the connection of spirit and soul in the perspectives of reason, for since the modern philosophy soul has been understood as reason, which is totally different from my suggestion that mind is the reflection of whole functions of our body. Now we are going to mainly review Kant, the synthesizer of rationalism and empiricism in the name of critique philosophy.

Kant says in the beginning of the preface of his *Critique of Pure Reason.*

> "Human reason has the peculiar fate in one species of its cognition that it is burdened with questions which it cannot dismiss, since they are given to it as problems by the nature

of reason itself, but which is also cannot answer, since they transcend every capacity of human reason."5)

Here he says about the dialectic character of reason; in his later verbose expounding, we can know the inevitable questions are about God, soul, and free will. Human reason has innate tendency to repeatedly ask about this existence; it means that above human reason there exists something mysterious which forces us to inquire about these beings. This can be one clue of reason to spirit.

Another connection of reason to spirit comes from epistemology itself; that is, without spirit we cannot know something because originally reason does not exist. What is called reason is in fact one of the faculty by which the soul under the spirit functions, only through which we can penetrate into the qualia of things. This fact can be known easily from the existence of sense organs from which we can define the synthesis of them as sensibility, of brain from which we can perceive coin concepts, and judge, which function is defined as reason, but beyond all of this faculty there should exist something essential and unique to humans, which can be defined as spirit, so it can make feeling, knowing, judging, and cognizing possible.

One more important clue of reason to spirit is that from ancient times all philosophies have had to deal with the matter of God the absolute being, but unfortunately human reason cannot go beyond the logic, so whenever it faces God, it always suffers from the inevitable fate of recognition or denial of God;

someone gladly receive God, but others definitely deny its existence. Of course skeptics have had the timid attitude of indecision.

But when we recognize the existence of God and presuppose that we are inherently spiritual beings, we can step forward to research the spirit, the most complicated but fruitful being. From this thinking we can review the historical movement of spirituality and contemporary research of spirituality as an interdisciplinary science.

Here many readers will ask me of the relation of spirit, soul, reason, understanding, and sensibility. In my long speculation about this, I will confidently say that human intelligence has the inevitable property of classifying, defining, and labeling everything around us, so that we have had many confused words in which all different as well as same connotations are included. Spirituality is pertaining to spirit; reason and understanding is to soul; sensibility is to body. All these functions are included in the faculty of spirit through the process of receiving empirical impressions by sensibilities, being arranged in the classification, definition, and naming by understanding, and being judged and conceived by reason. This is easily compared to computer with artificial intelligence, that is, computer hardware is human body, computer CPU is the soul, memory, calculation, and output of computer is reason and understanding; nevertheless we cannot say that computer has spirit because this is radically different from Aristotle's idea that the soul of ax is cutting, then is the soul of man knowledge? We cannot agree to his materialistic view at all.

Chapter 2: Human Being

Here we deny also Kant's unkempt thinking that soul is human consciousness. Kant's perspectives on the soul seems to focus on the epistemological truth; that is, he thinks human soul is just thinking ego which is not the same idea as many his former philosophers' thought about such everlasting being imperishable after one's death or something stood at the antipode of body. In his book *Critique of Pure Reason*, the Second Book of the Transcendental Dialectic, first and second chapter are dealing with the paralogisms of pure reason, in which the concept of soul has been researched very exhaustively in relation to the pure reason about why it continuously tries to go over the demarcation of experience and is vainly proud of knowing things in themselves and extend its range to the transcendental level of dialectics.

In B 399 of *Critique of Pure Reason*, Kant argues that a transcendental paralogism has a transcendental ground for inferring falsely due to its form from human reason, and will bring with it an unavoidable, although not insoluble, illusion. Kant infers that the concept **I think (the soul)** has been the inevitably problematic concept to go over the phenomenal world when perceiving myself as an object of inner sense.

In his opinion, soul is just the thinking subject, but the fundamentality of human soul as the reason cannot be justified if we exceed human experience, so the traditional idea about the simple substance, immortality of human soul should be denied; he says:

"Thus every dispute about the nature of our thinking being

and its conjunction with the corporeal world is merely a consequence of the fact that one fills the gap regarding what one does not know with paralogisms of reason, making thoughts into things and hypostatizing them." (A. 395)

He deals with the concept of soul from four angles: the substantiality of the soul, the simplicity of its quality, the identity of personality, the ideality of outer relation. He sees that from the wrong concepts of the soul there have arisen paralogisms of pure reason, which are in fact our illusions from our dialectical nature of pure reason, so Kant tries to disclose the contradiction of them, and demarcate pure reason within the boundary of experience to secure the safe region for practical reason to go forward.

But his concept of soul has been very controversial from the perspectives of traditional philosophers and contemporary thinkers. Above all, he expounds the concept of soul as the thinking ego, and this means that human soul is no other than consciousness based on human thinking in time structure, so seemingly his idea is very innovative by limiting human soul bravely in the boundary of experience, but from his conflicting idea of the soul, soul falls to the pitiless snare of materialistic view. In conclusion, Kant thinks that our soul is no more than the inner perceptions, and it has no real base in experience but only in logic it is possible.

For a long time, man has been defined as a rational animal, but in view of above argumentation, we cannot define man as a rational animal, because reason itself does not originally exist in the human consciousness as a soul; rather it has been established by being enriched abundantly in the human consciousness as a thinking ago; therefore the absolute criterion of reason cannot exist in the human thinking process, but this or that way reason has been interpreted as most important human characteristics without knowing its true origin. In my thinking man cannot be defined hastily as a rational animal without limiting its validity in the logical coherence of human cognizance; therefore we cannot dare verdict the validity of the above statement except the practical usage of our judgment in the total context of our knowing and applying it to the practical region of our cognizance.

IV. Materialistic View on Human Being

In modern times the materialistic propensity to conceive mind as the physical function of brain has been pervasive in many disciplines of the academic world; they even unfalteringly say that the mind is nothing but the brain, and man is no more than a material object having none but physical properties[6], so mental states are nothing but physical states of the brain.[7] From this daring confidence they develop their ideas about man, that is, man is a sort of material object. A man's body functions in a more or complex and curious way than any other known material object,[8] so they focus on the mechanism of mind without paying attention to human reason as the possible agent of making man know something, whether materially or spiritually; in this sense they are very daring materialists who can posit man in the state of material with no reason.

Here we are not in the position to discuss their thoughts detailed because of their huge volumes, but so as to focus on the theme of human reason, we need to briefly review their theory of mind. By grasping materialistic view, we can compare their thoughts to idealistic one, and afterward we can try to draw the whole blueprint of reforming society on some final concept.

In his book, *A Materialist Theory of the Mind*, Armstrong classifies theories of mind: mentalist theory, dualist theory, materialist theory.

Mentalist theory reduces body to mind or some property of mind like Hegel and his followers, who think that the whole material world is really mental or spiritual in nature, little as it may appear so. He thinks that Leibniz and Berkeley are also mentalists.

Dualist theory treats mind and matter as two independent sorts of thing.[9] In Dualist theory there are two main types: one is Cartesian dualism, in which the mind is a single non-material or spiritual substance somehow related to the body, that is, a person's mind is a single, continuing, non-material substance in some way related to the body.[10] Another one is bundle dualism, in which mind is represented as a bundle of perceptions as in David Hume. So the bundle dualist takes the mind to be a succession of non-physical particulars or items distinct from, although related to, the body. [11] Armstrong illustrates these two ideas by the distinction between in teractionist (a room and its thermostat) and parallelist (a room and its thermometer) theories. In interactionist theory, the body acts on the mind, the mind reacts back on the body, but in parallelist theory, they do not affect each other.[12]

Materialist theory strongly believes that man is nothing but a physical object, and so he is committed to giving a purely physical theory of the mind. In materialist theory there are two types: behaviorism and central state theory. The behaviorist denies that the mind is any sort of object, or collection of objects, arguing that to have a mind is simply to behave physically in a certain way, or to have tendencies to behave physically in a certain way. The central-state theory argues that mental states are identified with physical states of the organism that has the mind, in particular, with states of the brain or central nervous system.[13]

But some philosophers are not satisfied with central-state theory, so they espouse the identity theory, which suggests that the mind and the brain are identical. There is one more important theory which straddles between the dualists and the materialists. It argues that men, besides having physical properties, have further properties quite different from those possessed by ordinary physical objects. It is the possession of these unique properties that gives men a mind. This theory is called attribute theory.[14]

To this stage we have reviewed the materialist position about the theory of the mind with the book of D. M. Armstrong, but we will stop here to go ahead toward the cognitive science and artificial intelligence. The forward step to confirm that the mind is no more than the function of materialistic man is cognitive science. It aims at disclosing mind as the function of computerized man's brain. The fundamental concept of cognitive science is "that thinking can best be understood in terms of representational structures in the mind and computational procedures that operate on those structures." [15]

Cognitive science has replaced the crucial perspectives of rationalism by mixing interdisciplinary fields like psychology, neuroscience, linguistics, computer science, anthropology, sociology, and biology. In the cause of clarifying the secret of mind, it takes advantage of all kinds of truth but its orientation is physical science anyway. In cognitive science, functionalism is main currents, which suggests that mental states should be classified functionally. This means that mental states are not human unique characteristics, so any proper system of function for mental states can have mental states; in other word, non-human beings like animals, alien life forms, and even advanced computer can have mental states.[16]

Cognitive science focuses on analyzing cognition, not of the general essence or social or cultural touches of mind but of functional and physical system of mind, so it looks into the mind in the side of materialistic characteristics. Its dealing fields are: artificial intelligence, attention, knowledge and processing of language, learning and development, memory, perception and action, research methods, behavioral experiments, brain imaging, computational modeling, neurobiological methods, etc.[17]

Chapter 2: Human Being

Artificial intelligence is the most radical trial to imitate human mind into the computer system, by which contemporary communication industry has been developed so outstandingly that we cannot deny its huge influence on our everyday living, but when studying A. I. for this book, the detailed contents of artificial intelligence is shock itself. How can human mind be compared to machine intelligence? This has been possible on only materialistic thought about human mind which has long been supported by many renowned philosophers from ancient times. They have not cherished the nobleness of human mind and the possibility of spiritual existence at all. To save time I will briefly review the thesis of Aaron Sloman for expounding their thinking about A. I.

He presupposes that it is more fruitful to construe the mind as a control system than as a computational system (although computation can play a role in control mechanism.)[18] He suggests starting with the general notion of mechanism from traditional ideas of ancient Greek thinkers through modern analytic philosophers, for mechanism in response to environment can be the key point to the essence of A.I., but finally he reverts to the model of biological and mechanical system resembling human brain. He says:

> "The real determinants of the mind are not conceptual requirements such as rational-rationality, but biological and engineering design requirements, concerned with issues like speed, flexibility, appropriateness to the environment, copying with limited resources, information retention capabilities, etc."[19]

He thinks that human mind can be imitated in the form of A. I. on the design-based approach, which is paraphrased into a short phrase, *exactly like human mind*, so he definitely negates the existence of Kant's transcendental deduction.[20] His key idea is that a mind is a well-designed, sophisticated, self-modifying control system, with functional requirements such as speed, flexibility, adaptability, generality, precision and autonomous generation of goals.[21] He goes further to arguing that his idea of mind as a control system is basically different from conventional mathematical and engineering ones. In short, he thinks that a mind is an incredibly complex, self-monitoring, self-modifying control system, implemented at least in part as a collection of interacting virtual machines.[22] Based on this principle and tendency, he puts forward his hypothesis on the artificial intelligence and tries to establish its firm foundation by interdisciplinary scientific research.

Nowadays might be called 'the era of artificial intelligence' in the purview of materialistic view of man, so people could image all kinds of comfortable, speedy, and convenient way of living in near future thanks to the florid development of A. I., but to some extent mankind might have some fear of being ruled over by A. I. like Big Brother in George Orwell's novel, *1984*, because we could have a premonition that the most brilliantly developed computerized A. I. would obtain hegemony of the world and start lording it over the mankind in near future; in that case, A. I. would be the most flagrant disaster to mankind, and we would have no exit to escape from its merciless governing.

Chapter 2: Human Being

This pessimism might come from misinterpretation of Being, Human Being in the perspectives of human reason, so there underlies in our social conflicts and tragedies false concept of reason starting from the ancient Greek philosophy to the present Frankfurt school, so from now on we will review the concepts of reason and criticize them to find desirable base of society.

Chapter 3: Reason

The question about reason has been one of the outstanding philosophical themes, especially in the occidental world. Although there has not been any clear definition on the reason, generally it has been regarded as the faculty of principles.23) This means reason is the power to judge, infer, or systemize thoughts under the coherent rule. Normal persons are willing to admit this fact easily when looking back upon the grandiose achievements of human civilization, culture, and system, so it may well be conceived that these all have been possible thanks to the power of reason. In this context Aristotle's statement that the human being is rational could be justified.

But in contrast to this optimistic view of reason, contemporary times witnessed clearly negative attributes of human civilization toward destruction because of the instrumental nature of reason by which to extend imperialistic territories according to the unlimited greed. And in this context reason cannot be the sole substance of human nature in the highest standard of spirituality like divine love.

From these perspectives, all the sincere efforts to base social philosophy on the human reason would be futile, because their interpretation of human reason has been essentially prejudiced and partial from putting too much importance on Kant's and his German successor's interpretation of reason although their fluorescent development of idealism had ruled over the world in the form of political ideology, even to the

Chapter 3: Reason   55

Frankfurt School, so once being blocked off from the domineering protest of logical positivism, they had had no alternative except to delve and analyze language itself. But reason must be reinterpreted for the desirable reformation of society, because traditional interpretation of reason has been responsible for the present contradiction of human society from the beginning, but in spite of its false presupposition reason has shown off its brilliant achievement and glory in the civilization of human kind. In this purport, we are going to review traditional interpretation of reason and its extension to the contemporary fundamentality of the society.

Here we are going to review several theories of reason from ancient philosophers to the contemporary ones by focusing on their epistemological truth. So when we should review them, we can briefly summarize that reason has been equated with the most important faculty of sometimes soul, and other times mind, even spirit, so they cannot be differentiated easily, but Kant separated reason from soul completely, therefore finally reason was established within experience although reason was once regarded as human essence, and from him it has been imprisoned to the level of experience, so reason cannot go over the boundary of experience and this has made human capability of epistemological thinking to the narrow range of experiential science. After Kant, many important thinkers showed tendency that reason should be grasped as the material aspects, not related to the spirituality, and in contemporary days many philosophers like D. M. Armstrong suggested that human mind be no more than the material reflection of brain; even with time passage on, epistemological effort to clarify the origin and possibility of cognizing truth has mixed diverse scientific disciplines, even computer science and artificial intelligence (A. I) are now related to it, so that human cannot extend his idea to the spiritual fields although spirituality surely exists. Meanwhile, a newly arisen department of research for spirituality has extended its territory, so 'spirituality' is a concept that defines our era.[24]

Spirituality has been generally regarded as radically different from reason, but deeply looking into reason's property we can easily conclude that they might be closely related to each other, so we must review first the historical perspectives of reason, secondly German idealism focusing on Kant and Hegel, and thirdly we will review the negative perspectives on the reason from Frankfurt school.

I. Traditional Concept of Reason Before Kant

The concepts of reason, soul, mind, and spirit are very hard to distinguish between, for thinkers since ancient Greeks to contemporary days have used these concepts as the contrary meaning of matter and sometimes misused them without definite corresponding concept, so if we start separating their concepts at this stage, it will need a great space and has the danger to deviate from the main point, but for the clarity of our scheme, we need to focus on the concept of reason, so we will start from the ancient Greek philosophers.

Plato suggested that people's vulgar opinions be unclear

Chapter 3: Reason

and uncertain as collecting judgments, so they cannot be truth, and true cognition is realizing the idea of objects. But idea is reality, ideal, and prototype of individuals as the object to be grasped by intellect, not sensation. We can cognize something because of the reality of idea, and the most important and foundational of all ideas is the one of the good. Plato also suggested that human cognizance go through the stage of conjecture, belief, understanding, and reason, and reason should be the best way to cognize the domain of idea because by it we can get at the idea of the good most clearly.[25]

Aristotle says in *On the Soul* that reason is the form of soul which appears in the last stage of life development. Life starts from the plant phase with the basic principle of nutrition and reproduction and develops to the animal one in which sense of touch, emotion, appetite, and self-willed movement. Here finally comes human soul which uniquely possesses faculty of memory, conscious reminiscence. Reason is the form of thinking, understanding, cognition, and volition. Reason consists of passivity and activity, in which the former is the temporal one receiving form related closely to body but the latter is divine and eternal, therefore it is immortal.[26]

Since Aristotle, the concept of reason was not developed outstandingly once Christianity had seized the hegemony of the western world, but St. Augustine anticipated the principle of Descartes' philosophical maxim, *Cogito ergo Sum* (I think, therefore, I am.). We can ascertain this fact from his saying,

"The mind knows best what is nearest to it, and nothing is

nearer to the mind than itself. We exist and know that we exist, and have the existence and knowledge and on these three points no specious falsehood can deceive us......................for without any misleading fallacies and fancies of the imagination I am absolutely certain that I exist."27)

In the 13th century St. Aquinas found the genuine value of Aristotelian philosophy and applied it to his speculation. Aquinas thinks that reason is the divine power to differentiate human from animals because of the inherent capability of moral judgments. Reason is the control tower of understanding, judging, and acting what we are doing, so we should be responsible for our deeds and words before God, because we were granted the unique faculty from Him, so we must do all our actions according to our own free will given from God. Although we were born with various preferences and temperaments, and have been defiled by our sins, our responsibility for our sins has not been nullified because we have been led by our divine reason. He identified working of reason as the route to virtue, so reason can be the outstanding way of human virtues, so without reason human cannot be called human.28)

Modern era might start from the hot debate over the methodological way of reaching the cognition: induction and deduction. These two methodological ways of thinking are in fact their own confidence to find truth, but from Descartes we can see his emphasis on reason and from Locke, experience. These two antipodal logics are in fact both important for science as well as philosophy. But for our purpose of reviewing

Chapter 3: Reason 59

concept of reason, we must first see Descartes' thought about reason, and next we will review Locke as the founder of empiricism. Next we will briefly review Spinoza, Leibniz and Hume in the narrow range of their thought about reason.

Descartes started his philosophy from the existence of doubting ego, which is ultimately reduced to thinking ego, and as long as we think, we can exist, so thinking is the essential attributes of the human existence. His famous maxim, *Cogito Ergo Sum*. (I think, therefore I am.) can prove that one's thinking ego is one's mind, understanding, or a reasoning being. 29) And this is in another word soul and consciousness. In him, reason is the highest faculty in the soul, that is thinking ego, so all judgments and understanding come from reason. He thinks that thinking ego, the soul can be separated from the body. But his thoughts about soul are based on the natural scientific tendency at the time, and he supposed all thoughts be the reflection of the brain, so without limbs or any parts of the body, we can think.30)

Locke has been known as the founder of empiricism, but like Descartes he also conceives man as thinking self; nonetheless he develops his philosophy on the base of experience coming from ideas outside and inside ourselves. To Locke, the matter of mind, soul, and reason is centered on clarifying the origin of human understanding, so his research is focusing on the epistemological truth. In his thinking all knowledge is possible from the ideas arising from the sensation and reflection, so this means that he negates the innate ideas separated from our experience. He says:

"Let us suppose the mind to be, as we say, white paper, void of all characters, without any ideas:-How comes it to be furnished? Whence comes it by that vast store which the busy and boundless fancy of man has painted on it with an almost endless variety? Whence has it all the materials of reason and knowledge? To this I answer, in one word, from EXPERIENCE. In that all our knowledge is founded; and from that it ultimately derives itself."[31]

As regards to reason, he shows very negative attitude about it, because he thinks that reason is just the faculty of finding the means to justify that some propositions are certain and the others are probable. In his mind he has Aristotle as the person who justified reason from the syllogism. But he verbosely criticizes syllogism as means of reason to reach the truth.[32] To him syllogism cannot be believed the way to reach knowledge and truth. We can know about only some particular ideas by agreeing or disagreeing to them regardless of our reasoning and knowledge in our mind, so that the perception of the agreement or disagreement of our particular idea, is the whole and utmost of all our knowledge.[33]

Unlike Locke, to Spinoza God underlies in his all thinking system; so he develops his philosophy from the presupposition of God's absolute existence. To him the human mind is a part of the infinite intellect of God, and therefore it exists as God's externalizing idea, and as to reason, he distinguishes it from opinion and imagination and defines it as our possessing common notions and adequate ideas of the properties of things, and it is by the nature to conceive things not as contingent but as necessary, so it perceives things under a certain form of eternity.34) From this fact he can elicit the conclusion that the human mind possesses an adequate knowledge of the eternal and infinite essence of God.35)

Before finishing this section, we will briefly review Hume; he did not show particular thought about human reason, because he basically inherits Locke's idea with special emphasis on '*experience*' as the principle of British empiricism, but in fact decomposed it fully with his skepticism; even he denied existence of soul for the reason that we have only sensations and ideas as the weaker images from them or imaginations. He thought that a mind is nothing but heap or collection of different perceptions which succeed each other with an inconceivable rapidity and are in a perpetual flux and movement.36) As for the reason he cannot also depend on it because it is a kind of ungrounded belief without experience and observation. In a word, he was a skeptic who came to lose any empirical foundation at last.

Here we are going to stop reviewing more philosophers and start looking through German Idealism which has been regarded as the culminated theory of human reason, but fundamentally lacks more profound insights of human spirit, which resulted in inexpressible havoc on human destiny like Instrumental Reason.

II. German Idealism: Kant & Hegel

As a grand thinking system dealing with human reason,

there has been no rival against German idealism; especially in Kant and Hegel, the idea about the reason was culminated although their thinking systems had a lot of controversial argumentations. If we point out the important difference between Kant and Hegel, the former tried to limit reason to the range of human experience and demarcated the philosophy with theology, and adumbratively negated the existence of God, but the latter grasped working of human reason in the grand perspectives of world history as the process of revealing Absolute Idea. Kant researched deeply the limitation of reason in the epistemology but Hegel tried to show reason as divine function.

In his *Critique of Pure Reason*, Kant says proudly that he solved the hot debate between rationalism and empiricism, which were represented each by Descartes and Hume, over the empirical possibility of transcendental comprehensive judgment by Copernican revolution; that is, not to think of the object with reason but to think of it according to reason.[37] In Kant's view reason is the faculty giving the maxim of natural cognition, and pure reason is such that makes us recognize the rule to connote items innately.[38] Briefly speaking, reason is the faculty of principles.[39] But reason has basically inevitable destiny to solve the impossible questions, and with given conditions like intuitions from sense and concepts from understanding, it wants to enter into the transcendental world of idea, so it finally confronts the gigantic theological matters. He says that reason is no other than dialectical contradictions from which human tries to investigate the prime metaphysical principles like the existence of God, free will of human kind, and the immortality of human soul. But human reason cannot solve this matter at all, agonizing and finally giving up himself only into complacency in morality and religion. Kant recognized that this dialectical nature of reason is the inherent one deeply rooted in human nature.40) Here Kant criticizes reason's presumptuous suggestion of transcending the territory of experience and speculating on the ideal world; in other words he regards it just the transcendental faculty of human cognizance without being based on epistemological justification, so he thinks that if we transcend experiential world, we will plunge into the futile playfulness of our soul, thinking ego.

In his opinion, soul is just the thinking subject, but the fundamentality of human soul as the reason cannot be justified if we exceed human experience, so the traditional idea about the simple substance, immortality of human soul should be denied; he says:

> "Thus every dispute about the nature of our thinking being and its conjunction with the corporeal world is merely a consequence of the fact that one fills the gap regarding what one does not know with paralogisms of reason, making thoughts into things and hypostatizing them"41)

In his famous chapters, On the Paralogisms of Pure Reason, he radically circumscribe reason's region within experience, so the soul (thinking subject) itself should not try to speculate over the region of experience and should humbly kneel down before experience and should concentrate on human practical matter.42) Here on the epistemological deadlock, Kant gives up more research about the dialectical attribute of reason, and aims at negotiating transcendental philosophy with religion and morality, and call this practical reason. He thinks that practical reason is more needed than pure reason for the kingdom of purpose; in other word, human morality and religion cannot be proved their justification from the human pure reason, but it shall be necessary if practical reason can be their base. In conclusion Kant opened the gate of misunderstanding that reason has dual characters as well as dialectical ones: reason is the transcendental principle of cognition and at the same time the practical base of morality and religion.

In his masterpiece *Phenomenology of Spirit*, Hegel thinks that reason is the previous one of the final step in cognizing the absolute knowledge in the dialectical development stage of spirit. Consciousness develops from the world of sensuous certainty, which is the most uncertain and poor condition. Next it goes through understanding with inner self reflection on the object, transformed to the self-consciousness on the nature of object. Here self-consciousness becomes the reason by the dialectical unification process of the object and self. Self-consciousness immediately changes into reason, and so the negative relation of self-consciousness on the other being is soon transformed into positive one.43) Hegel thinks that reason becomes the inner self-consciousness through the unification of being in itself and being for itself.

Hegel says that reason is the confidence of consciousness

on that the ego is the reality of all things and being.44) The reason confident of being available to itself becomes the observant reason when confronting real objects, and realizes that the objects in the nature are no more than outer reason; that is, reason finds concepts or rule which are visualized in the inorganic nature. This rule is inner abstractness in thing-in-itself but at the same time principium found in reason itself.45)

 Hegel says that reason is alle Dingheit and the sheer objective Dingheit. But such is only available in the concept; therefore only concept is the truth of reason.46) This means that all things in the nature should be grasped in the reason when being subsumed in our consciousness, that is, through dialectical movement they become universal self-consciousness (reason) and finally spirit.

 Observant reason reaches the fulfillment of self-conscious realization in this free consciousness. Here reason as the concept reaches the stage of realizing the ethical and coexistent context with other people. Here two moments are being united as the virtues and world passage. So the deeds or criterion of individuality development become the goal itself.47) And they will be the two moments of rule making and its investigation and ultimately becomes immediate self-consciousness as the ethical substance. This self-consciousness becomes the spirit through the agent of reason, and it becomes the religion by way of modest personality, cultivation and enlightenment, the morality and moral world view. Religion is completed as the revelation one and becomes the absolute knowledge, when being and thinking are not separated but unified and thinking itself changes to its object. Now reason is identified as the same with being and what exists becomes reason and reality; therefore what is reasonable is real, and what is real is reasonable.48) Now reason reveals itself in the world history as the moment of self-realization which is being made in the history. This is slyness and the self-realization of reason. After all, the Hegelian concept of reason is the logical necessity to grasp Being including nature and spirit; that is, The Absolute, and inner law to reveal the self-development of Being, and this may be called as the completion of ideal reason concept.49)

Briefly speaking, to Kant human reason is the unclear inherent faculty in which boundary man knows something and act for something, but to Hegel human reason is the medium through which to know the Idea of the Absolute. But their incomplete interpretation of reason has been the inevitably tragic tools against mankind, from which all kinds of ideological conflict has arisen and still continue, and to this date has exerted very negative effect on human civilization; therefore with this negative perspectives, we will briefly review Frankfurt School from next section.

III. Frankfurt School

Nineteenth century might be dominated by the Hegelian thoughts, but in the twentieth century his philosophical system was attacked severely by almost all outstanding philosophers, but post the second world war, there arose another philosophical movement called *critical theory* which based on the criticism of German idealism. They borrowed Marxist philosophy for the oriented goal of social reformation with criticism of German idealism, so they researched reason critically and tried to base their philosophy on the most refined concepts of reason. We call them Frankfurt School, in which Horkheimer, Adorno, Marcuse, and Habermas are the heroes.

Philosophers of Frankfurt School grasped the concept of reason from the Marxian perspectives so as to establish the profitable social science of recompensing labor classes, but their researches have not clarified genuine essence of reason, only criticizing the social-economic inequality of the latter capitalistic industrialized countries. So we will review briefly their concepts of reason although they focus their research on material side like Marxist.

To them, reason is not profitable instrument of enlightenment and civilization but it is the instrumental reason, which became the base of fascism and totalitarianism in the latter industrialized capitalistic society and the terrible cause of bringing about disasters to mankind.

Horkheimer criticizes that traditional concepts of reason is the eternal logos without fundamentality, so modern society has been established by the false mathematical concepts of reason, but reason should be conceived as the foundation of critical theory for practical use of life. He thinks that reason can be formed when human determines subjectively, and this is very different idea from Kant, for he thinks that reason is formed first, and afterward givenness of sense and perception are decided.[50]

Horkheimer criticizes Hegel sharply also for the reason that Hegelian concept of reason is no more than ideal absolutization of subjective reason, not at all universal reason, so he cannot receive Hegel's thought that the Absolute goes toward the most reasonable world of purpose by revealing his slyness and finally realizes himself in the world history.[51] He thinks that reason is just the foundation of critical theory and clue to solve the contradictions of the society by which proletariat can enhance their living conditions in the material sides of equality. So we can say that his critical theory of reason is materialistic content of ideal concept of reason.[52]

Adorno thinks that reason has the innate negativity in its dialectical concepts. Originally Hegel thinks that concept develops dialectically in its negativity, but it goes toward the fulfillment of conceptual realization. Against Hegel's thinking, Adorno criticizes Hegel, because the fulfillment of conceptual realization by dialectical movement of concept is impossible, and it only moves continually in its negativity. He thinks that human history is little more than the dialectical movement of reason's logical self-realization, so in human history we can grasp all kinds of contradictions by the negativity of reason's inevitable attributes. In human society, reason has harangued eloquently to liberate man from the conquest of nature, but at final stage it made man subjugated by its inevitable property. This comes from the reason's unavoidable negativity, so contradictions of the society are the reflection of reason's dialectical negativity. But only reason can heal the society of all kinds of contradictions, for it only criticizes the society and puts forward proposals of its remedies. In this sense reason can act the foundation of critical theory, revealing its dialectical negativity in all contradictions of society. Here Adorno bitterly criticizes that in modern society man is being made the instrument of social institution when transacting his labor with master of production means. Here man has been sweated in their transactions of labor by the cunning of bourgeois's reason, so finally labor classes became subjected under the power of capitalism and humans fell to the instrument of capital owners. Adorno surveys the human history pessimistically from conceiving the logical development of negative dialectics of reason as fictional and human fall. So he puts forward that we should establish new social philosophy through critical self-reflection of reason.53)

To Marcuse, reason is also an important concept to form 'Dialectics of Negativity', but his concept of reason is the stronger momentum of economic, political, and social critique than Adorno's. In his thinking, Hegelian concept of reason seems to have fulfilled the harmony with the world, but in real world it is impossible, because real world sublates contradictions through confrontation and struggle incessantly. He thinks that Marxian view of real world is not the field of reason in which self-realization is fulfilled but the revolutionary momentum by which to negate the contradictions of the world, that is, dialectical power of negativity. He criticizes that reason already lost its power of dialectical negativity in the Comtian formal and dehumanizing concept of reason. He suggests that reason should restore original power of dialectical negativity, and exert the revolutionary power to rehabilitate humanity in the latter capitalistic society, because reason already lost its function from its formalization and instrumentalization.54)

Unlike Adorno and Marcuse, Habermas bases his philosophy on the dialectical identity of reason. In his opinion reason is the base of theory and practice, for it is the firm fundamentality of individual autonomy and happiness and maturity. To him constituent elements of reason mean will, consciousness, and liveliness; it means being reasonable according to its determination, so true cognizance is reaching self-reflection with interest in maturity by the presupposition of this reason. His methodology of social science is based on the dialectical identity of reason, which looks similar to Hegelian concept. As Hegel thinks that the self-realization of concept is fulfilled in the dialectical movement, Habermas supposes that the dialectical identity of concept is based on the self-realization of reason. He conceives the dialectical identity of concept of reason as the liberating epistemological interest in the linguistic and self-reflection process. He imagines ideal society founded on individuals from whose reasons man can liberate himself from social disharmony and contradictions in the effective communication of their wills.55)

To this stage, we have reviewed representative theories of Frankfurt school, but from now on we will progress toward criticizing reason as the fundamentality of our civilization, and by that we are going to seek for the desirable foundation of social philosophy.

IV. Critique of Reason's Fundamentality in Contemporary Civilization

Martin Luther once said that reason is a prostitute, but his saying was surely against the liberal tendency of interpreting Scriptures in the perspectives of human reason, in which there could be no truth and life of the Christianity, but in contrast to his stubborn objection to human reason, theological research has been focusing on the literary criticism which is supposed to have started from Schleiermacher, who based his theological philosophy on Kant's theory of religion in which all Christian religious events were interpreted on the base of human reason, so that since him theology has been the more subjected to the rational interpretation of biblical validity than ever. But we are going to focus on the fundamentality of reason that has underlain in the world, which aspects of civilization are no more than the reflection of reason in the present ongoing state.

In 20th century mankind experienced no more terrific and shuddering massacre than destruction of civilization. The fascist campaign for world conquest, which stands in the extreme capitalism and communism, forced all men to perceive in the cruel decimation that the demoniac Satan's sovereignty appeared. The use of aberrant cold reason in the ruling class ostentatiously displayed their flagrant power to make all human beings their slaves. Why was reason, which was once the object of respect and admiration in place of the idea of God for its integrity and excellence, degraded into a mean instrument of holocaust and demolition? Was really human reason fallen to the agent of retrogression and havoc rather than the one of leading man to progress and peace?[56]

The fundamentality of reason in the civilization of this world may well be criticized by the more intelligent and impartial philosophers, because its presumptuous self-display in the human history has left a huge havoc and insolvable cleavage to the world people and their way of living, so that we should analyze the problems of reason with cold and unprejudiced eyes.

First of all, reason has revealed its ambiguity of cognizing phenomena and noumena because of its transcendental limitation, in other word, with human reason we cannot see the reality of the thing, instead we are to look on the surface of the thing which has been caught by our faculty of sensibility and understanding, finally reason; therefore we cannot dare to say that we know something except unclear delineation of the thing; it may well be said that it is our destiny, then the struggle between empiricism and rationalism should have proved to be futile, because regardless of the abundant fruits of scientific research based on experiments and observation or the magnificent deduction system of proposition supported by only reason, the results of their fighting would be the same after all; this can be paraphrased briefly: Man shall not reach the truth of something by reason, for it is by nature limited.

This inevitably ambiguous limitation of reason might have brought about hot debate over the origin of the world: matter or mind, but how foolish may it have been if we have clung to the rotten rope of epistemology which has been doomed to be cut loose sooner or later, so we should look back upon the human history and search for the new way of reaching the truth as soon as possible; maybe it will be the better, the sooner it is.

But here we will not say it is due to someone's fault or neglect that reason has been enthroned in place of God in the name of humanities and held the hegemony in the civilization of human kind; rather we must concede that the negativity of reason has come from the innate destiny of human cognizance and the ambiguity of reason is a kind of inevitable limitation of human cognizance.

The second problem of reason is that it has acted presumptuously as the teacher of mankind; in other word, it has held the deep-rooted characteristics of leading and instructing people in the cause of edification, so that it has exerted almost absolute power on human culture in the cause of arousing people against the stupidity and illusion which are to result in unreasonable faith in the spiritual beings like gods, angels, and demons with continuously releasing fear and terror in the uncovered deep darkness and living tiptoe stance by looking beyond the unknown world of mystery; in this abyss of darkness humanists dared to say that only human reason can protect mankind against ignorance and fear of the natural world by means of science, and once the gate of nature was opened, all kinds of secrets and mystery of the world seemed to have been disclosed before human eyes, and men have been forced to be ruled by their powerful leading and dialectical teaching.

The eighteen century has been called the Age of Enlightenment because of the fecundity and splendor of the fruits of human reason, and at the same time leaving all value in the dust, reason has demonstrated its innate property of enlightenment to men; first of all, it tried to demolish the religious value of devotion to the absolute being, and liberated all immoral and lustful desires deeply rooted in the sensual instincts; from the result mankind was given the freedom of acting on their own judgment and will without being considerate of any supernatural being which could punish his actions if it be against its will and commandment.

According to Enlightenment Philosophy in the 18th century, in immature stage, mankind apotheosized nature with the sense of mystique and awe, soon imprisoned in them and forfeited in the form of worship, and in the course of living hard as slaves to the God, the hierarchy of religion became the shackles and whips to the people, so that human reason had to act as the demolisher of superstition and stupidity of mankind by finding the principles of nature and taking advantage of them by his own power of understanding; in this feat, the logical faculty of reason exerted great power on it, and operated on lineally without dialectic function of master and slave from any outside influence or inside hesitation and doubt.

But in 20th century, Horkheimer the leader of Frankfurt School saw that in the conflicting struggles of subject and object in the history of western philosophy, the subjective reason conquered the objective reason; in other word, they were united in the subjective reason by forcefully unilateral inclusion, and human history has run toward the passage to the enlightened world through the inveterate arrogant self-display of subjective reason; in this gloomy course, human reason has shown its underlain brutality in the enlightenment as the ideology of fascism and imperialism; we humans have acted on the pure calculating criterion of self sustenance only-that sinister wickedness was incarnated in the conquer, annihilation, and transplantation of race; war and self-deceit became the important means of self-justification, whether humane or inhumane, so that mankind fell to the last apocalyptic stage of shuddering in the massacre of mankind-this is the result of enlightenment of subjective reason. Horkheimer especially pointed out Kant and Hegel as the main figures whose misinterpretation of reason in the characteristics of enlightenment showed the insolvable dualistic division of cognizance as well as ambiguity of reason and as the instrumentality of reason.

Of course we have a lot of critique against the enlightenment of reason, but we had better stop here discussing it anymore; rather we are going to discuss the instrumentality of reason for the development of our total scheme. Originally this concept has been used by Horkheimer, the head of Frankfurt school, but his idea has been shared by his colleagues and soon it became his credited idea against the negative interpretation of human reason in the horrendous world war situation. Here we must review it first briefly and reflect on it by sharp eyes of criticism, because we are afraid of the terrible results of misinterpretation of reason regardless of its nutritious value for mankind.

Horkheimer deeply reflected on these modern tragedies and set out profound research to find out their causes, and recognized that those problems were originated from the limit of human reason's capability. With concentrating study on human reason in the western philosophy, he conceived that reason finally became the instrument and agency of destroying civilization. In this process he traced back through the steps and results in which the brutality of instrumental reason happened in the tradition of western philosophy with the method of scathing critique of human civilization. He discusses how the conventional concept of reason in western philosophy became the modern devastating property in the development of civilization, and how it led human kind into depravity, self-deceit rule of others, merciless extension of self-sustenance, and finally collapse.[57]

Horkheimer thinks that the enlightenment of reason has started from Kant's vague division of pure and practical reason because to Kant the ambiguity of reason has not been in harmony with cleft two regions of reason; rather man has supposed that for the well-being of humanity, the objective reason should yield to the subjective one, and if it be impossible, the forceful method should be lent and the illuminated light of reason should light on the world people for the purpose of guaranteeing the ultimate development and peace of the mankind; therefore his philosophy has enforced some bondage system to men in the noblest cause of utopian

Chapter 3: Reason

world, which could not be fulfilled in human world by any means. The enforced system of reason on society has been developed into the means of ruling over the suppressed and lording it over the inferiors of human groups.

In my thinking, the Kantian epistemological establishment through the fundamental systemization of pure reason has become the base of practical reason, but under the fundamentality of enlightened world, Kantian ambiguity and dualism has been laid, and this philosophical systematic oppression is no more than the basic fascistic thoughts of totalitarian illusion for utopia. In the society reason unifies the universals (society) and particulars (individual) in the cause of fulfillment of totality for the functional aim of self-sustenance; in the ultimate it swallows both and becomes a monster, that is to say the instrumental reason; therefore self-sustenance and self-destruction has been overlapped deeply, revealing the contradiction because of the meaningless system of pure reason. Now the artifice of sly reason for self-sustenance was completely transformed to instrumental reason, and the ruling class throws hypocritical slogan of utopia, aiming at the fascistic power sustenance, and individuals also dedicate themselves to only one purpose: self-sustenance, so that they are willing to do wickedly against their conscience.[58]

When reason does not contribute to the enhancement of human morale and sovereignty, it shall be the devilish instrument of doing away with humanity and healthy well-being based on the peace and harmony; in this sense, reason should have been applied to all fields of human life, but limitless avarice of man has taken advantage of the excellent faculty of reason, exerting its power on extension and occupation of self territories from inferior material desires, so that nowadays human reason has gotten to be defiled to the degree of being unable to be healed and restored. This can be called the ultimate crisis of reason without any prospect and possibility of expecting the most brilliant glory which was once conceived as the reasonable and inevitable road of reason.

To this stage we have discussed about critique of reason's fundamentality in three directions: ambiguity, enlightenment, and the instrumentality, but we come to realize that these three are intermixed with each other in the negative substance of reason; especially in the Marxist interpretation of Frankfurt School, which had tried to set up the progressively capitalistic society based on the Marxian materialistic view of the world; to their eyes reason cannot be the cornerstone of desirable society, because it cannot be built upon the problematic human reason; however, they had overlooked one crucial point, that is, without reason we cannot know something although vaguely and without it we cannot act on some moral foundation; then without reason, where can we elicit the justified grounds of our human ethics in the society?

After all, we must start from analyzing another positivity of reason for building up moral standards; then we had better go over to discussing positive aspects of human reason as the merging junction of human knowledge and morality. So from now on we are going to discuss human morality in the positive perspectives of human reason.

Chapter 4: Morality

The morality of man has been one of the important theme in the history of philosophy, oriental or occidental, and it has been studied in the name of ethics. Without morality man shall be the animal of no reason, because it is one of the most striking characteristics of mankind; generally morality has been believed to have come from the property of reason, but this has not been proved regardless of a lot of research on the relation of reason to morality; therefore we should not hastily conclude that the morality is the product of human reason and we should delve deeper into its validity.

There could be many questions regarding the morality, but the most important question should be what is the essence of morality in the perspectives of the first principle of morality, in which we can suggest firstly the unity of knowledge and the conduct represented by the ancient main oriental philosophy and Socrates, and secondly social justice in Plato, utilitarianism and contemporary Rolls, thirdly pursuit of happiness in Taoism and Aristotle, fourthly divine love of Christianity, fifthly existential action of contemporary existentialists, finally imperative categories of Kant. The second question should be what the relation of reason and morality is and how morality can be elicited from the reason in the analysis of its nature: practical reason or pure reason if the division of reason into pure and practical reason can be justified.

Answering all these questions shall be a great burden to us, but that should be necessarily studied and replied because it is so much urgent that we cannot go forward to establishing better social philosophy without it.

I. The Essence of Morality

Generally it is said that man only has the morality in his communal life, but this is very foolish thinking, because in the nature all kinds of animals have their own forms of moral although it seems instinctive, but here we must think that human morality has some transcendental value different from the ones of animals; that is, in human morality we can see the unique characteristics of human integrity and divine endowment, which is essentially distinguished from the instinctive ones of animals. But once starting our speculation on what is the essence of morality to human beings, we cannot easily define it as something, because there shall be many difficult questions which require prompt reply; for example, is it a kind of inner voice of our heart? Is it the best judgment to consider myself including others? Is it the enforced social norms which to follow guarantees our security and well-being but in opposite case, it will bring about the serious punishment? Or is it the established customs and manners which members should follow regardless of its validity?

The genesis of morality might be from the supernatural wisdom of the so-called saints or heroes with the noblest consideration of might-be the common well-being of some community; in this sense in the oriental world saints or great monarchs were supposed to establish the morals for the society, and they had been stored up into the magnum opus scriptures and forced people to follow unconditionally without their justification; so that in this oriental world, morals were kinds of mixture of preaching, commandments, laws, and even social customs and manners. In this sense the morality in the orient was believed to aim at the well-being of maximum range of the whole people of the society, in this point it can be compared to the utilitarianism of western world.

(A) Unity of Knowledge and Conduct

Almost all of ancient oriental teachings of human morality focused on the unity of knowledge and conduct, so regardless of their fundamental difference of their doctrines they unanimously taught that ethical knowledge without conduct would be futile; therefore their teachings were emphasizing being a good man in the family, community, and the country, which means that man must be contributive to their own society by the unity of knowledge and conduct.

Among many oriental teachings, Confucianism has been regarded as the summation of human morality in the society. The Confucian scholars presupposed 'Tien' (Heaven) as the supreme origin of human morality, and this is similar to the concept of God in the Christianity without having personality but having been grasped transcendentally as the ultimate Being in the universe, and this Tien endowed man with the sense of morality through nature, therefore we can immediately understand and know what is right and wrong in the judgment of our action, but this action based on the morality should be occurred after having get over the natural instincts and returning to the ultimate morality, and they called this 'Re' by which man can do anything without violating the morals of the essential human property, and the man who achieved the final stage of 'Re' is called a noble man, and he only has the qualification to rule the household, country, and the world.

The Confucian scholars also have presupposed 'Nature' as the foundation of human morality which is believed to have come from Tien, so that it is the inborn capability to have morality in human consciousness. They think that from this nature there arises mind which has four fundamentals: the mind for sympathy, the mind for shame, the mind for concession, the mind for discernment. From the mind for sympathy there arises mercy, from the mind for shame, righteousness, from the mind for concession, manners, and from the mind for discernment, wisdom. From these four fundamentals there happen seven emotions: joy, anger, grief, fear, love, hate, and desire. In the 15thcentury, Hwang Lee one of the greatest Korean Confucian thinker, once said that the four fundamentals come from the innate human nature which equals the Lie of matter, and seven emotions result from the endowed properties of human personality which equals the Ki of matter. But his opinion had been argued intensely by many Confucian thinkers regarding the function of Li and Ki in human mind, so that to this date the argumentation has not been settled yet. But striking fact about the Confucian thinkers, many o f them reached the highest stage of controlling their minds to the degree not to be moved by any outer temptation

Chapter 4: Morality

of sexual desire, worldly fame and wealth, in other word, they were morally perfect in mastering their hearts.

In Buddhist ethics, they aimed at the Nirvana in which they were liberated from the mundane karma, forgetting their egos ultimately and compassioning all beings surrounding them. This stage can be reached by training Noble Eight Path: righteous sight, righteous thinking, righteous speaking, righteous deed, righteous livelihood, righteous training, righteous awakening, righteous meditation. From exercising these ways, man can reach the Nirvana, which is the supreme degree of realizing the reality of being, and after this stage, man should serve the poor and weak without being considerate of one's profit, which is called Journey as a bodhi sattva. From this purport the Buddhists regards self-forgetting as the supreme principle of their ethics and Schopenhauer borrowed this concept for the base of his moral philosophy. I will discuss this point in the next section in which we will discuss critique of Schopenhauer's moral philosophy.

In the ancient Korean Three One philosophy, man should stop the sensual feeling, should deep breathe, and should keep himself from touching outer world, paying attention to one will to correcting wrongs and recovering truth, finally a great identity of true divine form appearing and reaching the ultimate stage of a saint who can know true reality of the world and act for the well-being of the common people. Their morality was focused on living in this mundane world, ruling reasonably, and serving men for their maximum well-being, and this is called 'Maximum Well-Being for Men'.

In the oriental world these ethical essences were mixed knowingly or unknowingly, merged into peoples' lives this or that way, so that distinguishing from which ethical essences had influenced outstandingly could not be possible although main effects on different peoples could be differentiated from some main characteristics of their national lives or cultural heritage. But this theme in the oriental philosophy had better not be discussed any longer here, because of its too wide and deep contents as well as too limited space of this book; rather we will go over to the western philosophy.

Socrates has been regarded as the father of western ethics, who turned around from the materialistic tendency of the era investigating the natural world to establishing morals of human beings in the polis; therefore his major concern is man, especially man's wisdom, which starts from 'knowing yourself' like the inscription in the forecourt of the Temple of Apollo at Delphi. He identified the knowledge of oneself as the conduct toward the well-being of the community, particularly Athens; he did not pursue the selfish happiness; rather he focused on the total harmonious well-being of the social beings, therefore his ethics is no more than the practical application of uniting knowledge and conduct. Here naturally we can have questions, "Why did he emphasize that knowledge of oneself should be presupposed to conduct?", "Did he mean without knowledge (wisdom) we cannot conduct toward the well-being of the polis?", "What is the foundation of uniting knowledge and conduct?" These questions seem to have huge connotations in themselves and also have the danger not to be justified by any philosophical pursuits, because knowing oneself is itself impossible to reach the stage; rather we must confess that we do not know anything, and we are living in the illusion and self-conceit, so that all false consciousness has flown into our inner hearts continually to the final stage of our death, which means the liberation of the misconception of self-deceit and terrible prejudices colored by our own tastes, preferences, desires, instincts, and inevitable bondage of human ego. In any sense, Socratic pursuit of wisdom and action in the real world would be destined to fall because of its innate contradictions, but his ethical attitude toward Athens' people were really grandeur itself, because in his heart he already hug them as his brethren whose existence was not the object of curse and overthrow but the one of enlightenment and guide toward the paragon of man whose direction had been already prescribed by gods who were believed to live everlastingly in the eternal world, and man should follow their ways to go over to the living of permanence; in this sense Socratic ethical question were the method to excel human limitation and enter the kingdom of gods which were invisible to human eyes but in the human soul it would be grasped. The self-awareness of one's ignorance, hearing one's inner voice, and conducting wisely and positively in the polis by unselfish motive were the Socrates' characteristics of the principle of morality.

(B) Social Justice

In contrast to the principle of uniting knowledge and conduct, some philosophers think that establishing justice in the society should be the first principle of ethics. Among them Plato is outstanding in ancient philosophers and the utilitarians are in the modern days represented by Bentham and Mill.

Plato thought so radically about the ethical questions from witnessing his idol teacher's innocent death by seemingly foolish pubic who got the hegemony in the democratic system, so his ethics is focusing on establishing justice on the republic by four virtues for each class: wisdom for rulers, courage for guardians, temperance for producers, and when these three virtues work in harmony, which means that each class does one's part well, the state will be in harmony and the justice works in the country. But this simple idea originated from his analogy that the state is the same as human, so human justice is paralleled to state justice, that is, the reason for the soul is inferred to the wisdom for rulers, the spirit for the heart to the courage for guardians, the appetite for the body to the temperance for producers.

But this analogy seems to be very unreasonable, because his analogy of man's function to the one of the state is a kind of fallacy of prerequisite; in other word the man and the state are originally different, so that his enlargement of human function to the one of state cannot be justified, and man's justice cannot match the one of the state. His Greek word for justice is, δικαιοσύνη but this word connotes 'morality' or 'righteousness', so that man's justice means in any sense man's duty to the community in which he belongs; then we must abide by our duty to the community, and this has the very conflicting views of individuals to the society; i.e., if one has urgent private duty to one's parents who must be supported by their child, but the state summons one because of the urgent defense against the invaders, how can we act in this situation? Should we desert our filial duty to our parents and follow nation's order to participate in the fighting camp against our enemies? Or should we give up nation's order to take care of our parents in this situation? Some say that the loyalty to the state is superior to the filial duty, but we can doubt whether the state would guarantee our parents' safety when we fight against the invaders fiercely without being considerate of our lives or parents.

In Plato's concept of justice, he overlooked the most important point, that is, the individual's true well-being, because his philosophy focuses only on the totality of the society, not paying attention to the individuality, so that when he admired Spartan virtues of forgetting individuality and devoting to the totality of the state, he must have overlooked the most important principle of human individuality and heralded the rise of totalitarianism in mankind, first in Greek world, next papacy, fascism, and communism, and maybe his ethics would be taken advantage of by some sly guy in establishing Big Brother's society ruled by the most supreme artificial intelligence, therefore we need to criticize his ethics more attentively than ever and just look on favorably his good will to establish rule of philosophers.

Although utilitarians aimed at the greatest happiness of the greatest number of those affected and had personal happiness at heart, their thinking labeled utilitarianism cannot guarantee private happiness as the ultimate moral principle because the final destination of their idea would be the totalitarian happiness of society by which the social justice can be attained; from this results there has arisen a lot of debate over the danger of their idea. Among them, the biggest problem is whether society can overlook personal immoral actions in the cause of utilitarianism; for example, whether or not to promote the maximum happiness of the maximum number of the society men can eliminate serious criminals at will; if most of the people in some society eagerly want to kill drug dealers mercilessly without being judged by the judicial system, can such action be justified by human morality? In the perspectives of utilitarianism, deleting such criminals can be validated for the greatest happiness of the greatest number, because the total pleasure of the most of the people minus the total suffering of them shall be surely bigger than not deleting them. This is very dangerous thinking, because on the base of utilitarianism, fascists and communist had massacred enormous innocent people ferociously, and we have witnessed such terrible scenes in the world history.

The second problem of utilitarianism is if there is such means to measure the amount of pleasure minus suffering from all pertained to the moral actions because it requires consequentialism; however, happiness in each person has each degree of satisfaction from outer or inner sources, so that one's

Chapter 4: Morality

happiness is surely relative; nevertheless utilitarian's suggestion of maximum happiness of maximum number would not be reasonable at all, which can lay the just firm base of totalitarian dogmas. The problem of quantification in utility is impossible to be justified from the beginning of presupposing utilitarianism as the moral principle; nevertheless utilitarians have tried to set up the elaborate system of theory to apply to the morality of everyday living.

Although Mill deepened utilitarianism from the emphasis on quantity of the pleasure in the moral actions to introducing the quality of the pleasure in it, all moral actions cannot be calculated despite every means possible, so that the firm base in the utilitarianism cannot be found in the quantification as well as qualification of pleasure in moral actions; which means their metaphysical trial to explain the principle of morality has proved a failure. Pope John Paul II expressed his objection to utilitarianism against its making persons the object of use when he said, "Utilitarianism is a civilization of production and of use, a civilization of things and not of persons, a civilization in which persons are used in the same way as things are used."[59]

The other complex argumentation for or against utilitarianism would be more necessary to expatiate, but except its noble purpose of establishing social justice by the moral principle of the greatest happiness of the greatest number we should look into its great peril by which to lower men into the object of utility and think little of individual humanity, and it shall not be the desirable moral principle to advance social justice, so from now on we are going to discuss other theories of the first principle of morality; in which pursuit of happiness has cut a conspicuous figure, but divine love also has been acted most powerfully since those Middle Ages in the name of Christianity; while stoicism was once popular in the high groups of intelligentia for so short a time, and in the age of reason Kant's grand system of morality represented by categorical imperative had effected enormously on men. After him we have never witnessed such a magnificent system of moral principle as the supreme universality to be applied to all mankind; since the end of 19th century only before the serious crisis of human collapse, existentialists have thought only existential actions were needed to break loose the wall of existence, but their moral principles were theoretically weak in comparing one of previous peaceful era; but in consideration of connection to next section we will continue to discuss the essence of morality in the order of pursuit of happiness, divine love, existential action, and categorical imperative.

(C) Pursuit of Happiness

The goal of morality cannot be espoused only in the noble cause of the unity of knowledge and conduct for the cause of social security and development, for man is not only the social animal but also the solitary one who pursues one's own happiness; in this sense many theories have appeared on the history of philosophy, but still oriental Taoism and Aristotle has been regarded as the great achievements of happiness theory for the human morality, so we will start from Taoism.

Chapter 4: Morality

In Taoism, they embodied Taoist hermit as their ideal man, who forgets all worldly meddlesome matters and enjoys one's life in the maximum satisfaction, so that they are being united in the natural world without trying to change it. They regularly practice deep breathing, exercising martial arts, taking in special medicine to extend their longevity, sometimes drinking alcoholic beverages and dancing freely in the beautiful scenery, finally reaching the stage of being one with the nature. In some sense, Taoist ethics can be conceived as selfish one, because it focuses on one's supreme well-being, not on the social relations, so that they negated the complicated social manners like Confucianism, emphasizing that the state should be small and the ruler should not do any artificial policies for the citizens; rather the state must let them alone, and people will be wealthy and happy for themselves, because it matches the principle of the universe, that is, inaction nature.

Taoism has been very influential to the oriental world as the main practical ethics to this date, and its importance is still getting bigger and bigger, but in the western world Aristotle's influence as the moral philosophy has not been so much big as Taoism; nevertheless his magnificent theory shown in Nichomachean Ethics cannot be negated against its excellence. Aristotle pursues moral philosophy starting from defining personal happiness as the ultimate goal of man with being always in the middle path, but he also puts forward social justice as the most important task of man. His moral themes are so wide and deep that we cannot deal with them easily in this small space, so we are going to focus on only criticizing his too much optimistic view of life in treating morality of man. In Nicomachean Ethics, Aristotle showed too optimistic view of life, and this seems to be contrary to his image as a cold and analytical versatile philosopher who is superb in all kinds of scientific discipline. We don't know where such his views came from, but by analyzing parts of his ethical idea, we can pursue his thoughts in the ethical perspectives of a humanist.

Aristotle starts his discussion about his view of human life from three types of life: the life of gratification or pleasure, the life of active citizen (or statesman), and the life of the philosopher (or scientist). To these three types of life he attributes different properties of life in view of what is the highest good for their life goal. He sarcastically criticizes the life of pleasure which is eagerly wanted by normal persons by comparing it to the one of cow, and upgrades the life of active citizen to the level of regarding the highest good in their lives as the esteem from others, especially from the intelligent people in order to prove that they are the good men. Here he skips the discussion about the properties of philosophers and starts his lengthy discussion about the highest good and ultimate goal in life and a prosperous life. In his thinking wealth cannot be what is the highest good thing, because 'the good' should guarantee what provides the reason for doing all the other things, but wealth can be just a means to something else, so it cannot be an ultimate goal. So he says:

> "And a goal that's *never* a means to anything else is *more*

ultimate than the ones that we value *partly* for their own sake and *partly* as a means to something else. And a *purely* ultimate goal is something we *always* want for itself and *never* as means to something else."60)

Here we can know that he infers the connection between what is the highest good thing and a prosperous life; i.e., he is now suggesting that the ultimate life goal is a prosperous life. From this step he progresses toward its definition. He says that prosperity is what we have needed for its own sake, not as a means to something else, but 'having all you need' should be in the context of social level in consideration of our families, friends, acquaintances, and even fellow citizens because we are social animals. As for his position, we can clearly understand from his own conclusion:

"So here are our conclusions: to prosper in life is our ultimate goal; it implies having all you need; and it's the goal of all our actions."61)

For explicating his suggestion, he discusses human tasks by proposing that we can work how human beings prosper *by working out* the task or function of a human being. He assumes that we prosper *by fulfilling our function* ― by doing what we are made to do. But this tasks are not [merely] expressed in our physical function like growing and reproducing; he denies even the animalistic perception in human tasks, so he naturally leads his main points to make all this clearer, in the same way to the life of the rational part of us: a life of action, which means a life of exercising of our [rational] capacities, that is, a life of exercising the soul and of rational agency, and there is a *further* point: that we must perform our function *well*; hence, as *good* human beings; *with goodness*, so a good man do this task well honorably based on its goodness. Here he confidently concludes that the highest good for human beings is the exercising of the soul in accordance with human goodness for the whole set of human virtues over a full life time.

To this stage he has shown his optimistic view of life in that he thinks his ethical foundation is possible to approach, and the exercising of the soul in the practical life is easy to fulfill. But in contrast to his view, life is so much complicated as to grasp in the simple ethical sense, and the mind of usual people is not so easy as his suggestion, and we have been forced to be impressed so strongly about his ignorance of usual people's heart and the complex reality of human life from his description of his ethical philosophy; he sees human life as too easy, simple, and formal to penetrate into the essence of human personality and its extension to the social life. Of course he develops his logic gradually from human ultimate goodness and his goal to prospering life and the life of exercising soul as a social animal. He even furthered that a prosperous life is the best thing, the most honorable, and the most pleasurable.

But then he turns rounds his attention to the purely external events which can influence and damage human life full of prosperity and tasks of soul: he says that prospering requires external goods as well and it is impossible to do honorable things without material sources. This is very serious change of perspectives because to this stage he has exclusively emphasized the importance of the life task of exercising our soul. When we carefully read his suggestion, we come to understand his presupposition that there lies uncertainty inevitably in our lives caused by our need for external resources. He says:

> "Life is full of sudden changes, and all sorts of strokes of good and bad luck, and even the most prosperous people can suffer terrible tragedies before the end, like King Priam in the Iliad; and if someone experiences that kind of misfortune and ends his life miserably, no one would say they'd prospered."[62)]

Though conceding the role of chance or luck in our prosperity, Aristotle denies their ultimate influence on the prosperity of human life; rather he suggests that real prosperous person deals with misfortunes honorably and can prosper for the whole of his life. He suggests that a good person prosper over whole life in dealing with the outward vicissitudes with imperturbability and dignity. Aristotle thinks that when we handle a series of misfortune calmly without being hurt by such bad situations and by exercising our virtues in that way a prosperous life can continue. So finally he reverts to his original optimistic view of life. But it is as if he came away from it, then goes back.

When we compare his position in the Book 3 in which the bravery is discussed in great detail, we can know he keeps his somewhat pessimistic view of life, because he says that the goal of bravery is actually something pleasurable and brave man should endure wound and pain in the crucial dangers to keep honor and evade shamefulness. So when he says below, he shifts from the adamant optimistic view of life to somewhat pessimistic view:

> "In fact, if he's a good man in every way, and therefore prospering in life, dying will be all the more distressing for him, because a man like that has so much to live for, and he'll be conscious of the fact that he's being robbed of the greatest blessings-and that's painful."63)

Here we can again know how much Aristotle thinks much of life, and from his attachment to life we can find that he continues to conceive human life as the most valuable one to live by although it sounds tragic seemingly that the brave man dies in pain and distress and loses everything. In contrast to Socrates he shows his detestability of death and his attachment to life-this is believed to have come from his unconditional optimistic view of life, but in dealing with the bravery he has changed his coherent position as the optimist of human life to slightly gray pessimistic view of life, because although we love our lives very much, we must face death-this is really an inevitable tragedies of human life.

To this stage we have reviewed Aristotle's optimistic view of life from the Book 1 of Nicomachean Ethics and chapter 9 of Book 3, and we clearly come to believe that his view of life has stood in the only bright side of life although he mentions some dark side of life, so from now on we will criticize his optimistic view in the existentially phenomenological way.

Briefly speaking, Aristotle's optimistic view of human life is the ethics of the strong and powerful. It may fit the standard criterion of formalized ethical life, so his ethical thoughts might have been the canonical philosophy of the Catholic Church in the Middle Ages. This can be analyzed from his lack of understanding normal or lower people's lives which are the most part of humankind. Maybe it comes from the fact that he was by nature pertained to upper classes whose lives could be totally different from normal or plain people's lives. In fact as a son of court medical doctor, he was educated under the best teaching of the great philosopher Plato and taught Alexander the Great, one of the greatest kings in the human history, and after his death he slightly suffered from persecution, but he managed to operate his own academy and lived peacefully for the whole lives, so in his thinking we cannot find his deep understanding of normal people's lives.

From above description about his life background, we can guess his ethics could have oriented toward the very noble aim of human life, but from now on we shall go forward to criticize deep-rooted problems of his ethic in his optimistic view of life. So first we had better criticize his position from his classification of human lives to three types: the life of gratification, the life of the active citizen, and the life of the philosopher (or scientist). This classification cannot be justified because his presupposition has some unproved formal ways. Existentially we cannot say that we have some definite ways of lives, because to justify his classification the human life we have to ask about its essence first. What is a human being? A social animal? No, that is a very simple grasping of human essence. It is a very particular perspective. An animal with reason? No, that too is very formalistic way of expressing human essence: in intellectual function only. So if he cannot define human beings correctly, how can he proceed to the definition of human life? Why does man live? For pleasure like normal persons? For recognition like statesman? For seeking truth like philosophers or scientists? All his classification seems to start from his psychological sense of superiority over all people because he was a court philosopher who couldn't experience the sufferings and hardships of normal persons.

The division of human life to three types may be irrelevant to his social position, because as a humanist he classifies it on the base of human being without considering it related or connected to God. So in any sense he was a faithful humanist who viewed human life not from the eyes of God but from the humanity itself.

Existentially we might think that human life has no definite way or goal; rather it is formless or chaotic in every way of our lives, so we have witnessed all kinds of evils, massacres, chaos, and disorders in human history, so regardless of Zoroastrianism's teaching about the existence and struggle of the good and evil, we can see all kinds of bad things and heinous misdeeds in everyday living; we cannot be assured of peaceful lives in our living despite the superficial rest and the unprecedented development of our technologies.

Why do we have innate unrest and worrying about our destiny and inevitable solitariness in our hearts? If he had

Chapter 4: Morality

discussed these psychological phenomena clearly and then proceeded toward the analysis of classification of the ways of human lives, we might be able to agree to his argumentation to some extent, but his ossified classification of the ways of human lives cannot be justified at these chaotic days of human history, for in his ethics he does not seriously discuss the existence of the evil and good and their disharmony and conflict in our heart, so his account of human life as the optimistic one lacks the function of the evil and all kinds of human irrationality.

As regards to his thinking connection of what is ultimate good, the goal of human life, and a prosperous life we can criticize his position as too much optimistic view of human life. If we existentially analyze it, human life appears not the good thing with the definite goal for prospering life. If we look around our surroundings, we can see a lot of tragedies from the ordeals of our life: suffering of the birth, decrepitude, sickness, and death. Everyday living of our lives has been full of worrying, anxiety, fear, conflict, etc. As Buddha once said, life is the sea of suffering. We can see all kinds of evils and flagrant iniquities around our surroundings which we cannot imagine. We have all kinds of ordeal from our inner struggling against our insatiate sexual wishes, immorality, vainglory, and unsearchable pursuit of our spiritual object — all these things eloquently say that our lives do not have an ultimate good or a simple, definite form of prosperity. According to Aristotle, we should pursue the finality of having satisfaction from all needs, but it was a kind of illusionary dreaming like Karl Marx and his followers. So his ethics should be criticized from his too much optimistic view of human life which can be summarized like this: he thinks that we can attain unlimited human prosperity armed with best virtues in unison with our family and friends over our whole life time. Of course in our thinking we can state it like that, but in reality at this era most of people are groaning from lack of money to sustain themselves and their families, so from the initial time of our birth on this earth we cannot expect any prosperity in our lives; even we cannot set our eyes on our definite goal of life because at any moment the burdensome tasks of our lives cannot liberate ourselves from all kinds of hardships, so with what the ultimate good, can we expect our lives should be prosperous? Like Jean Paul Sartre's saying, we are surrounded by the existential wall, so we have had no escape from this harsh reality. Then, how can we agree to Aristotle's too optimistic view of human life?

Although Aristotle opened the new gate of seeing human life with the positive and hopeful perspectives of a prosperous life as the definite goal with the ultimate goodness, we cannot easily agree to his ethical thoughts for the reason that it is too much optimistic view of human life to have the firm ground of phenomenological analysis of human lives; rather it could be the court ethics to lead all people to some visualized ideology of prosperity. From this innate advantage, it could become the standard philosophy of the Catholic Churches in the Middle Ages, but when analyzing his thoughts in view of existentially phenomenological method, his thoughts should be criticized against its too optimistic views of human life and its too formalized ideas.

From above position, first of all we can criticize his classification of human life as the very vulnerable one which is not based on the reality of normal or lower people by pointing out that his presupposition of human life lacks fundamental understanding, so we need to define human and next human life as X and after that we can classify what types human lives have.

His focus on a prosperous life with the goal by ultimate goodness cannot be justified also by the existentially phenomenological method of analyzing human lives, because by nature human life seems to have no formal way or goal of life seeing on the base of human tragedies; in other word human life has not oriented toward the desirable way in contrast to Aristotle's and other thinkers' expectation.

Unlike his emphasis on exercising of the soul for a prosperous life, human soul has run toward the chaos and self destruction in all kinds of evils, misdeeds, and heinous massacres from terrible hatred against each other. So however radiant human development may be in the technological and industrial fields, human destiny lies ahead in the uncertainty and pessimistic future, so Aristotle's brilliant but too optimistic view of human life cannot be applicable to this era of chaos and uncertainty.

(D) Divine Love

Although stoicism contributed to the private ethics, it was very narrow ranged and self-centered morality, so that it could not be positioned as the desirable social standard of moral, for it only focused on one's inner peace and harmony in the soul, giving desirable contentment to the followers, but ultimately it was inclined to one's self-complacency; therefore its influence on the Mediterranean territories of Roman empire was not so serious as Christianity.

Christianity has been regarded one of the most controversial religion in the human history, but in view of human ethics, it has had its own share in the development of human morality, therefore we are going to discuss just the effects of Christian ethics on man, not on the religious doctrine.

Among all ethical doctrines of mankind during the process of world history, Christian ethics might be called the most difficult to practice but easiest to know; the reason is that knowing is one and doing is another; in other word, man has failed in their moral achievements because of man's incapability to do some righteous thing, not man's capability to know something.

Christian ethics is summarized as following Jesus' word:

> "Love the Lord your God with all your heart and with all your soul and with all your mind, and Love your neighbor as yourself."[64]

Seemingly these two great commandments are impossible to practice; firstly we haven't been confident of the existence of

God and we have no knowledge of God; furthermore loving God with our all might looks very unreasonable, because we must sustain ourselves first above all things; furthermore loving our neighbor as ourselves seems void, because we cannot love even our families heartily, so that the peremptory saying of Jesus looks so contradictory that we cannot practice them at all.

Christian ethics is based on these two commandments of loving the God and our neighbors, and all other commandments and directions are subjected to these two creeds with which man can be determined to sacrifice himself in any situation, and the power from true love of God and neighbor can get over all the other circumstances, but that is the supreme level of Christian ethics, in which man can be united with God and neighbor and feel blissful from God in the special power from outside of us; it is the Holy Spirit, which is believed to have come from the God and Jesus Christ after his ascension to the Kingdom of God.

In Christian ethics men are all sinners before God, and we cannot be justified before God at all, because in our hearts we are full of all evils: sexual immorality, impurity and debauchery; idolatry and witchcraft; hatred, discord, jealousy, fits of rage, selfish ambition, dissensions, factions, and envy; drunkenness, orgies, and the like.[65] Living on this earth equals being defiled by sinful nature, but with our will and practice we cannot overcome our sins because by nature we humans are beings of fallen estimates, so even though somebody seems good and noble in his heart, distinguished from his colleagues, he is the same as his friends in the sight of God, because there can be no difference in their sinful natures, small or big, so that only God's grace can be the cure-all of our sins, and his grace appears in the form of Holy Spirit which can be experienced only when born again.

In this sense Christian ethics is the emphasis on God's grace through faith in Jesus in true heart, and then Holy Spirit comes upon true believers, encouraging, chastising, and guiding our spirit in our prayers, reading Holy Scriptures, praise, evangelism and mission, and helping the poor and weak; this ethics is not the morality of the weakling like Nietzsche's saying, for he misunderstood the essence of Christian doctrines as the fallen and rotten morality of the materialistic persons. Love means not weak and poor condition; rather it is the highest level of human morality, because human cannot be lowered down to the demons or animals of the law of the jungle, but he parallels devilish superego as the paragon of true superman who can neglect all boundaries of the good and the evil, so that acting against the general rule of morality was praised as heroic deeds to be able to achieve the mission impossible, and in his eyes all the hierarchical system of western Christendom was already in the deep crisis of destruction and hopelessness; maybe he had a premonition of the collapse of western civilization in the state of godlessness.

(E) Existential Action

Generally existential thinkers have considered that

Chapter 4: Morality

existence precedes essence[66]. What this means is that human kind should focus not on essential nature of thinking but on life itself. Since Descartes' famous maxim, 'I think, therefore I am', western philosophers have concentrated on finding the essence of human thinking, so the main theme of philosophy has been the theory of knowledge. But from the dismal fin de siècle symptoms, existential philosophers paid attention to human tragedies, and what mattered was not essence of our thinking but existence itself of human kind.

Dusk portends night, and dissents bring about struggles in the end. After watching long shadow of cursed putrefaction of Christendom over the human history, Nietzsche foreshadowed the dark history of human existence filled with wars, hatred, betrayal, self-contempt, long groaning from absolute solitariness, and holocausts. Nietzsche became the forerunner of dissenters and traitors against God, so he dared to proclaim "God is dead."[67] as the representative of them. If something absolute occupying our soul disappears, something more excitative should come next. Nietzsche must have been unrestful and terribly lonely, so he had to be assumed mad, because he could not sustain his soul in the world without God, so he tried to penetrate into the genuine characteristics of our lives and establish the new value toward which we should orient. In his thinking, the autocrat God disappeared, so new power had to appear on the scene of human history, but it was not easy matter, for God was once omnipotent, omniscient, and omnipresent, so in the world of his absence we had to sustain ourselves by our weak ability and wandering conscious selves.

Here he suggested the 'Superman', who is above the demarcation of good and evil and can do whatever he thinks necessary, so he is the master of himself, and he does not need to be approved by the inherited values or morals, only his judgement can be his criterion. Here, we can guess how much thirsty Nietzsche had been in the unrestful state without God; therefore, he emphasizes the independence of our soul from all handed values of human history, especially Christian morals which he had cursed as weakling's one.

Sartre can be called an heir to Nietzsche in contemporary days, because he proclaimed publicly that God was dead, but unlike Nietzsche he was seemingly not mad, and looked not lonely, for he emphasized the importance of human solidarity as the valuable foundation of human existence. When we analyzed his deep personality, we could find how much he was problematic in his state of soul. As an atheist, he acted as a resistance and communist in the Second World War, watching human horrors everywhere, thinking the futility of human pursuit of epistemological truth starting from Cartesian maxim, 'I think, therefore I am.' To him, existence is the most desperate matter, not the idea of truth (essence). Of course he knows that by Cartesian method we can attain our thinking selves, but it is not our requisite matter in this troubled world; rather it just leads us to subjectivism, from which human beings could fall to atoms, and could not establish the desirable world.

Without God, Sartre also puts forward the independence of human soul from all handed-down values or morals. According

Chapter 4: Morality 107

to him, we cannot expect any wise or appropriate judgment from all our preserved moralistic criteria when we face the inevitable decision like the case of deciding between tending lonely mother or serving country militarily in the cause of world peace. He sharply advises us to decide for yourselves, because we are the destiny of our existence, to which anybody or any beings cannot send any profitable help. In this sense, in the world without God, we must be independent of all established values or morals, for we are by nature free. So the fighting for freedom requires us action. Here action means not the passive but positive one to reach one's own freedom and humanity. In explaining existentialism, he defines the humanity as the universal value for which we should act. He says,

> "What is at the very heart and center of existentialism, is the absolute character of the free commitment, by which every man realizes himself in realizing a type of humanity."[68]

Similar to Sartre, as a communist Camus lived the flame-like life to fight against two super powers of totalitarianism represented by the USSR and the USA for a whole life. Officially he denied himself as an existentialist, but he stressed the absurdity of human existence. As an atheist, he thinks this world has been full of absurd condition, especially human lives are paradoxical ones between two conflicting values: happiness or unhappiness, meaningful life or meaningless one. In his book, *The Myth of Sisyphus,* he shows that in the situation of no God and absolute truth, man's search for meaning is useless, but this absurdity cannot justify our suicide; rather we should revolt against such absurdity although the result would be terrible tragedy like Sisyphus in the Greek myth. He leaps his suggestion to creation of meaning, which is not a viable alternative but a logical leap and an evasion of the problem.

In his book, *the stranger*, he shows us how much man could be absurd in the real action and attitude in our living situation. Life is itself absurd but irresistible. From hero's unreasonable and immoral actions, we can see the upcoming absurd world full of insane men and women who think themselves victims of this terrible world without God or absolute value or morals. So from Camus' perspectives, living itself should be circumscribed by the absurd existence of human beings. We don't know God; neither do we need God, because our lives are full of absurdity; rather we should fight against the evil powers of the world. But in spite of this absurdity we should object to the nihilism, because it's ok to have the process of fighting against the nothingness like Sisyphus. He says,

> "If nothing had any meaning, you would be right. But there is something that still has a meaning."[69]

Finally Camus thinks much of such concepts of cooperation, joint effort, and solidarity to overcome the absurdity of our living, so we need rebellion as the basis of human solidarity.

To this we reviewed the most important elements that constitute a meaningful life from the renowned existential thinkers Nietzsche, Sartre, and Camus. In briefly speaking, they are 'autonomy' (Nietzsche), 'freedom' (Sartre), and 'revolt' (Camus). But the concepts are intermingled so complicatedly that we cannot easily differentiate them. But one thing is outstandingly clear, that is, they might have struggled spiritually for the human freedom in the atheistic situation which had been full of all kinds of tragedies, terrors, absurdities, cruelties, and holocausts.

When I reviewed their ethical tendencies, I could find that they were by nature spiritually independent, who had disliked authority itself and eagerly wanted to stand up by only human power. In any sense, they represented the contemporary situation briefly labeled 'chaos', from which post modernity has witnessed all kinds of nihilistic and apocalyptic symptoms of evils and depravity. From the traditional classification, we can conceive them as the heirs of Dionysus rather than Apollo.

Darkness precedes light, and as yet darkness presides over all the universe, which is assumed mostly pertaining to dark power. So our lives could be full of darkness without God, from which all conditions might have flown; then how could we adjust ourselves to this existential situation full of meaningless recurrence everlastingly?

Next we are going to deal with the most formal theory of morality established by Kant, which has been known categorical imperative and it has been supposed to come from his meritable negotiation with pure reason to enter the realm of purpose represented by the morality and religion, but this theory does not seem palatable to us because of the abstruse and difficult terms and content. Nevertheless we should go forward to understand and criticize his theory of morality to full context.

(F) Categorical Imperative

Kant's Categorical Imperative is thought radically different from other philosopher's point of view. We can infer that Kant emphasizes the ultimately universal law of morality which is expressed by formulae of categorical imperative, and Kant finds his base of moral philosophy from the reason. As we see, Kant have pursued the universal principle of moral philosophy by turning around from the pure reason to the practical reason, so he wants categorical imperative to be the cornerstone of his moral philosophy, and the five formulations of categorical imperative are kinds of practical application of the universal and abstract principle to the concrete world of morality. Categorical imperative is conceived as Kant's most important conception of moral philosophy. Kant starts expounding this concept from suggesting that the moral philosophy should be metaphysics of morals which origin should be found in the pure practical reason.[70]

Kant thinks that we should act according to the objective principle in the nature as rational beings, and it is our will which is nothing other than our practical reason.[71]

From his definition we can know imperative is a kind of formula of absolute command of reason, and categorical imperative means that its end is objectively necessary without referencing to any other end. In other word, there can be no other purpose in commanding one's action than ultimately final order of morality. Kant says this point clearly;

> "The categorical imperative would be that which represented an action as necessary of itself without reference to another end, that is, as objectively necessary"[72]

Here before going over to five formulae of categorical imperative, we should know first of all how categorical imperative is possible. As for this question, Kant expounds it in the last section of his book *Groundwork of the Metaphysics of Morals*. In brief, we are pertaining to the world of understanding (reason) and at the same time to the world of sense (desire and inclination). Then, all our actions are being made from our will with some end and synchronically some means, which is our volition of autonomy. If our actions are corresponding to the pure law of reason, there would be no problem, but as the being is always affected by our sense, our actions would be oriented freely toward the natural instinct; here in the conflict of our morality and freedom, our actions should be unconditionally matching the supreme law of morality which is deduced from a priori synthetic proposition; this is the categorical imperative.

But in order to apply this categorical imperative to the practical laws of our actions, Kant expresses it by several formulae, which are expressed as a priori synthetic practical propositions.[73] So from this universality of the formulae of the categorical imperative, one's maxim of actions should confirm to the universal law unconditionally. Kant suggests five formulae of the categorical imperative: the formula of universal law (FUL), the formula of humanity (FH), and the formula of the autonomy (FA), and from FUL he adds the formula of universal law of nature (FUL/N), and from FA he adds the formula of kingdom of ends (FKE).

The formula of universal law (FUL) is expressed as this: *"Act only on that maxim whereby you can at the same time will that is become universal law."*[74] This formula is the basic one of all formulae. The understanding of FUL is that whenever we act, our maxim of actions should be matching universal law, which means that our principle of actions must be based on what can be applied to universal standards; in other word our action should have the criterion to which all human beings can agree, and there cannot be any exception and deviation from the moral principle itself. And this FUL is slightly transformed to FUL/N in the sense that we human beings are pertaining to the general law of nature although we are confident that we are free from all our surroundings, we are forced to be part of the nature and our actions based on our maxim must be corresponding with universal law of nature.

Then, what is the function of this FUL/N in doing our real duties? If an agent formulates his self-interested maxim, then his maxim should pass through this FUL/N. Kant exemplifies this formula from four examples, but in consideration of space, we can explain it from the case of the needy man who promises to pay back money with no intention to.

The man knows that his situation is too urgent not to borrow money, and it is impossible for him to pay back. Before borrowing money, he is struggling between his conscience and desperate situation, so he is forced to make his self-interested maxim so as to borrow money, and soon asks about the possibility of the universalization of his maxim. But he reaches the conclusion that his maxim should be universalized and borrows money by the promise to pay back although he visualized the result would be his breaking the promise in the universalization of his maxim. After all, his promising would be no credible to all because his maxim of self-universalization is contradictory to the universal law of nature; in other word, he failed in the test of FUL/N. Kant sees the universalization test as having the effect of ruling out immoral maxims, so the positive duty is a result of this "negative" dimension of FUL.

The formula of humanity (FH) is about the objective practical laws to which our actions must be necessarily matching the end of our will. In other word, whenever we act, our will of actions should be corresponding to the a priori synthetic end, because we humans are rational beings who must be regarded as the absolute end, not means. Kant expresses this objective practical law as the formula of humanity in the categorical imperative. It is: "*So act as to treat humanity, whether your own person or in that of any other, in every case at the same time as an end, never as a means only.*"75)

Here we need more detailed expounding of this FH. According to Kant, human is a rational being who can act by his own will for the end which must be matching the objective practical law.[76] Here we can say that human being and every rational being exist as an end, not means, so we must always treat them as ends because they have absolute worth, not exchangeable price. So Kant asserts clearly: *rational nature exists as an end in itself.*[77] From this absolute value of humanity as rational beings, formula of humanity comes about.

This FH can be the objective practical law of our morality, for human being has absolute worth not comparable to any being in the universe, because as a rational being he can will freely based on his reason. Here we can suppose that if all human beings have absolute worth because of their rational property, we must concede that all human beings have the same absolute worth like me, then they cannot be neglected or taken advantage of as means; but unfortunately in human history we have witnessed that human beings have been treated as means to attain to such goal as such set up by dictatorial leaders or heinous groups like Nazi, so from Kant's this FH we can expect some advanced moral philosophy by which all human beings can be treated as end itself, not means.

For explaining this FH, Kant illustrates the meaning of FH from two examples: the needy man who borrows money from friends without intending to pay back, and the wealthy person who enjoys himself but do not help the poor. The former case is surely for the needy man to use other human as means, so it is clearly violation of FH, but the latter case is not the same as the former one. Although the wealthy person does not help the poor, this does violate FH, for Kant says that not helping others would only harmonize negatively, not positively, with *humanity as an end in itself*[78]; in other word this is negatively away from achieving the common humanity as beings of ends.

From these two formulae FUL/N and FH, Kant elicits the practical principle of the will from the universal practical reason. Kant systematically shows us how Formula of Autonomy comes about. First, FUL/N can be deduced objectively in the rule, which is the universal law of nature. Second, FH is elicited subjectively in the end, which is an objective end rooted in the pure reason. From these two principles there arises the third practical principle of the will which is the ultimate condition of its harmony with the universal practical reason. These three formulae are connected mutually in the universal practical reason. Kant describes this third formula FA as following: the idea of *the will of every rational being as a will giving universal law.*[79]

This FA shows us clearly that our morality is founded on our autonomy of the will; in other words, all our moral actions come from our free will based on our pure practical reason whenever we act on our maxims which must be matched to universal law of nature in consideration of humanity as the end itself.

Finally, Kant has inferred that as a citizen of free will (autonomy), I am pertaining to the community of which constituents are unanimously regarded as ends, not means because they are all free citizens who can determine their maxims on their own autonomy, but they must be corresponding to the universal law of nature. Here there arises automatically the conclusion that we must act on our own maxims of autonomy in consideration of others as ends, which must be harmonious with the ultimate principles of morality, so from this inference the formulae of Kingdom of Ends (FKE) comes about, and it is expressed as this: *Act according to the maxims of a member of a merely possible kingdom of ends legislating in it universally.*[80] Professor Larry Blum expresses FKE as easily as possible like this: *All maxims ought, by their own legislation, to harmonize with a possible kingdom of ends as with a kingdom of nature.*[81]

Although the language expresses diverse function of the formulations of our categorical imperative in five different formulations, all moral laws have the fundamentally same origin in the pure practical reason, so Kant first shows the diversification of our maxims in a form of consisting universality, a matter of an end and a complete determination of all maxims of harmony with kingdom of ends. But this diversification should be converged into the ultimate formula which concludes all five formulations in one absolute categorical imperative. Kant expresses this fact clearly. "*Act on maxims which can at the same time have for their object themselves as universal law of nature.*"[82] In next sentence Kant says this is the formula of an absolutely good will.

To this stage we have interpreted Kant's five formulae of categorical imperative, but from now on we are going to discuss the relation of reason and morality; then we need to start from analyzing validity of Kant's categorical imperative as the universal principle of morality. Among many philosophers against Kant's ethics Schopenhauer has stood striking in the

Chapter 4: Morality   117

opposite side, so we are going to start from Schopenhauer's critique of Kant's categorical imperatives.

II. Relation of Reason and Morality

To this stage we have delved most important theories of essence of morality in the influential thinkers, whether religion or philosophy, but in the development of ethics, the relation of reason and morality has been revealed outstandingly related to each other, so in any sense, human reason is no more than the fundamental base of morality, but this suggestion has shown so vulnerable weaknesses when asked the validity of reason as the base of morality, because most of the philosophers have thought that reason has both sides of theoretical and practical ones, so when it would be applied to the epistemological truth, it should be grasped as the foundation of truth of knowledge, but when it would be applied to human morality it should be transformed immediately to the practical reason as we have seen the case in Kant's *Critique of Practical Reason*. This seems the same in Schopenhauer's moral philosophy, because he also hadn't distinguished the cleavage between two properties of reason: theoretical or practical one. Generally in western thinkers practical reason has been labelled as the base of human morality without having proved any legitimate division between theoretical reason and practical reason; therefore we must obtain the truthful base of their division as the foundation of morality, and we should doubt whether reason shall be the base of human morality like Schopenhauer, who has coherently criticized Kantian moral philosophy which is believed to be based on so-called practical reason and put forward new idea of 'compassion' as the base of morality although in his moral philosophy he adulterated his concept of compassion with theoretical reason as the foundation of morality.

Here we had better review why Schopenhauer passionately criticized Kant's categorical imperatives as the universal law of morality and whether his purview of human morality with basing on emotional feeling is really worth to reconsider the validity of human moral standards.

(A) Schopenhauer's Critique of Kant's Categorical Imperatives

In the introduction of his book, *On the Basis of Morality*, Schopenhauer summarizes his overall view of criticism against Kant's moral philosophy, focusing on Kant's categorical imperative. The main point of Schopenhauer's criticizing Kant's moral philosophy is that Kant's categorical imperative of practical reason has no objective foundation in the human nature. He definitely proclaims that so-called *moral law* doesn't exist at all, so he sublimely sets out to prove that Kant's moral philosophy based on this categorical imperative of practical reason is a kind of false assumption. He says:

> "I therefore confess the particular pleasure with which I set to work to remove the broad cushion from ethics, and frankly express my intention of proving that Kant's practical reason and

Chapter 4: Morality

categorical imperative are wholly unjustified, groundless, and fictitious assumptions, and of showing that even Kant's ethics lacks a solid foundation."83)

In Chapter 4 *On the Imperative Form of Kantian Ethics*, from this perspective Schopenhauer begins attack on Kant's ethics as falling in a positive *petitio principi* because it already presupposes the validity of our moral laws, so Kantian ethics is founded on what is called objective moral law; it is the categorical imperative of which true identity has not been proved but posing as an absolute being, so Schopenhauer criticizes categorical imperative as unreal. Instead, he proposes the law of motivation as a form of the law of causality; in other words, human do some actions on his own will by the law of motivation as human is part of nature. Schopenhauer criticizes the absolute necessity of the categorical imperative for the reason that there is no way to prove the absolute necessity, so until it is proved we cannot introduce the moral law into our scientific ethics.

In addition to the invalidity of moral laws, Schopenhauer tirelessly objects that Kantian ethics represented by the absolute moral law, which is expressed as categorical imperative, is elicited from the theological morale, that is, Decalogue (Ten Commandments). In Schopenhauer's thinking, the ethical imperative form of *du sollt (though shalt)* is a kind of law, commandment, and obligation (duty) based on the Decalogue, and Kant's categorical imperative was unknowingly influenced by it. So when Kant says theological hypothesis that there is absolute ought and unconditioned duty, he already commits a *contradictio in adjecto* (contradiction in the adjective); this means that there cannot be 'absolute' ought or 'unconditioned' duty, because the two adjectives, 'absolute' or 'unconditioned' cannot be posted before the two nouns without being proved for their credentials; they are no more than products of Kantian theological hypotheses. Schopenhauer says this clearly.

> "But from theological morals Kant had borrowed this *imperative form* of ethics tacitly and without examining it. The hypotheses of such morals and hence theology really underlie that form."84)

According to Schopenhauer, before Kant, this imperative form of morals had been used in moral philosophy as a doctrine of duties, but Kant's giving the foundation on the moral philosophy as the imperative form, it became exceedingly omnipotent doctrine of which base shall not need any more research.

In chapter 6 *the basis of the Kantian Ethics*, Schopenhauer goes ahead briskly in criticizing Kant's moral philosophy against mainly two points; the first is that the basis of moral law, that is, categorical imperative has no substance because so-called moral law is nothing more than the a priori synthetic form which comes about from the pure reason, so this moral law is just the mere skeleton of human cognition without any empirical foundation. Schopenhauer poignantly penetrates into the hidden secret of the categorical imperative by revealing its contradiction as a form of phenomenon of the pure reason

Chapter 4: Morality

and its inevitable connection to the thing-in-itself which cannot be validated at all as the moral principle. He says:

> "Accordingly, if also in practical philosophy his alleged moral law originates a priori in our head, it must likewise be only a form of the *phenomenon*, and is bound to leave untouched the essence-in-itself of things. But this conclusion would be wholly incompatible with the fact itself, as also with Kant's views. For everywhere it is precisely *what is moral within us* that he describes as being in the closest connection with the essence-in-itself of things, in fact, as directly touching this. Even in the *Critique of Pure Reason*, wherever the mysterious *thing-in-itself* stands out somewhat more clearly, it proclaims itself as that which is *moral* in us, as *will*. But this he disregarded."[85]

This universality of the pure form of our morality as categorical imperative abstracts all empirical motives of the will, objectively or subjectively, and aims at only the conformity to the law itself which is applicable to all regardless of its previous validity or deduction.

The second point is that his main concepts of '*duty*' and '*categorical imperative*' as the basis of all moral actions are in fact another paraphrase of '*ought*' which origin comes from theological morals. This is the intensification of his criticism against categorical imperative in the chapter 4. He clarifies this point by saying this:

> "But as the word *respect* cannot have been so inappropriately put in the place of *obedience* without a good reason, it must indeed serve some purpose, and this is obviously none other than

to veil the derivation of the imperative form and the concept of duty from *theological* morals."86)

Schopenhauer also criticizes a group of Kantian philosophers against their thoughts of Kant's categorical imperative as a fact of consciousness although Kant excludes the possibility that categorical imperative should be moral law coming from the moral consciousness which is no other than empirical resources, whether outer or inner; especially he criticizes that Fichte's calling Kant's categorical imperative as an *absolute postulate* means his falling into the *petitio principii* like Kant himself.

Here if we briefly summarize Schopenhauer's criticism against Kant's categorical imperative, it is eloquently expressed in this short sentence, that is, "that origin of a moral law within us is impossible."87)

In his thinking, Kant's categorical imperative lacks the pre-proof of its existence because it has no basis in the experience of human consciousness or will with some motivation; rather it is a kind of mere thought process which foundation cannot be found anywhere but shows off its absoluteness or universality.

At this point, he thoroughly delves deeper into Kant's categorical imperative in the perspectives of the above negative two reasons in the unprecedentedly long one passage from page 74-76 of *On the Basis of Morality*. In this one long passage, Schopenhauer pours his painstaking criticism against Kant's categorical imperative; especially on its lack of real foundation as the moral principle. In other word, he concentrates on his criticism against Kant's categorical imperative with the conclusion: *Therefore the second defect in the Kantian basis of morality is a lack of real substance.*[88)]

This conclusion is originally elicited from his tough objection to Kant's idea that the categorical imperative originates from practical reason, because he thinks that the categorical imperative of practical reason is the law that results from the thought processes.[89)]

When we review his opinion carefully, we come to know that he thinks Kant's categorical imperative is very problematic because it is no more than the law of the thought processes; that is, it is just formality of morality void of any content. He expounds his position with two points: The one point is that there can be no moral law in us, for if there is a moral law within us, it automatically directs a law for our will, but if it is just thought process like Kant's suggestion, how can it rule our will? So Schopenhauer thinks that for a law of our will, some impetus and occasion is necessary to us; this means that without specific instinctive moral law human doesn't act. The another point is that because of Kant's wrong suggestion of categorical imperative, which is no more than thought processes, empirical and egoistic motives of the moment have been the main moral law for long time; in other word, in contrast to Kant's intention, his categorical imperative, the skeleton thought processes just has contributed to the wrongly directed development of moral philosophy. Further explaining, Kant's categorical imperative lacks all empirical and concrete reality, and it allows us just 'egoism' as moral law.

He emphatically argues that so as to move one's will, the moral stimulus should be 'real' to the level of announcing itself automatically and positively, for only empirical existence has reality for man; this argumentation is the emphasis on the importance of empirical moral stimulus and motive for the reason that human morality is concerned with not the a priori building of houses of cards but with the actual conduct of man,90) but Kant's categorical imperative looks like building a web in the air from its void.

Schopenhauer furthers criticizing Kant's categorical imperative against its originality from abstract, pure, and a priori pure reason and its applicability to human beings and all rational beings. But it has no concrete foundation in reality because of no empirical content. Here Schopenhauer reaches the conclusion in the beginning of this paper, and proudly boasts that there have been few philosophers who could realize the serious weakness of Kantian moral philosophy based on categorical imperative; in this showing off we can guess Schopenhauer thinks he has been the only philosopher who can point out Kant's crucial weaknesses in his idea of categorical imperative.

Schopenhauer poignantly argues that Kant has imposed great burden on his categorical imperative, namely the hypothesis of the freedom of the will, and Kant consistently suggests that freedom cannot occur in the actions of man, and theoretically it is not possible.91) But Schopenhauer disproves Kant's idea that freedom can occur in the noumenal necessity of duty and performance, which is no other than categorical imperative, because what is not possible is also not actual, so we must reject Kant's categorical imperative as the postulate of morality before building false doctrine on another.

In his thinking, Kant's saying, "the moral law is, so to speak, a fact of pure reason."[92)] is a dogmatic suggestion of which validity cannot be obtained at all in human cognizance. His emphatic criticism against this dogma is really well expressed in these sentences.

> "On page 83, R. 164, we also read of "a reason *directly* determining the will," and so on. Now it should here be borne in mind that in the *Foundations* Kant expressly and repeatedly rejects every anthropological basis, every proof of the categorical imperative as a fact of consciousness, because such a proof would be *empirical*."[93)]

Schopenhauer analyzes this dogmatic assertion of Kant into finding that Kant identifies virtue as coming from pure reason and they are melted together into one and the same, so that pure reason unknowingly transforms to practical reason and it gives birth to the categorical imperative as universal law of morality. But here he criticizes Kant's unity of pure reason as the foundation of practical reason as presumptuous misuse of reason; he even radically refutes the German idealists like Hegel because they pushed pure reason to the level of comprehending even the supersensuous (thing-in-itself) and the Absolute. He suggests that Kantian categorical imperative comes from rational psychology which origin is from Plato through Descartes to Spinoza, Locke, and Kant. Their dualism about the function of material body and immaterial soul is the fountain of Kant's rational psychology, from which categorical imperative shows off its birth certificate, but it has no substance and should be refuted from the scientific ethics.

This is the summary of Schopenhauer's criticism against Kant's categorical imperative to chapter 6, but he tenaciously continues charging his attack against Kant's categorical imperative in chapter 7 and 8. So from now on we are going to briefly summarize his sharpened criticism against Kant in the formulae of categorical imperative.

In chapter 7, he concentrates on attacking mainly Formula of Universal Law (FUL). Here he criticizes that FUL is not yet moral principle itself but only a heuristic rule for it, in other words, an indication of where it is to be sought.94) This means that FUL is not yet the supreme moral principle but is the only sign by which to find it. He thinks that the maxim itself in the FUL is the actual moral principle, for willing is real base of our actions, but in connection to actions of our will, Schopenhauer strongly supposes that in Kantian moral actions egoism lies as moral principle. His thinking can be summarized in his saying, "I can will only *that* which is to my greatest advantage."95) In his thinking moral obligation rests on reciprocity, which can be working in the compromise in view of egoistic calculation, if not, it will be revoked immediately.

From above mentioned facts, Schopenhauer determines that Kant's fundamental rule of morals is not categorical imperative but in fact a *hypothetical* one.96) This means that FUL cannot be the supreme moral principle because of there

Chapter 4: Morality   127

being no absolute real foundation and conditional rule of egoism. Schopenhauer clarifies this point:

> "In the previous section it was shown that Kant's supreme principle of morals lacked real *foundation*. Closely associated with this defect and contrary to Kant's express assertion is its concealed *hypothetical* nature, by virtue of which it is even based on pure *egoism*, and this is the secret interpreter of the instruction given in the principle."[97)]

Instead of FUL, he puts forward a proposition as the true and genuine substance of all morality: "Injure no one; on the contrary, help everyone as much as you can."[98)]

Against this positive principle of our morality, he digs up the dark side of our nature coming from our innate egoism, citing, "Help no one; on the contrary, injure all if it brings you any advantage."[99)] He thinks that getting over this egoism and malice should be the task of all ethics.

In the last part of chapter 7, he criticizes Kant's moral principle of two duties: the duties of law and the duties of virtue. He suggests that the former cannot be conceived as a universal law of nature, and the latter can be conceived as the one but cannot be willed, therefore Kant's two duties of law are contradictory to real world in view of the case of suicide. Kant's two duties are in fact denying a natural law as moral principle. Here Schopenhauer shows off that his moral principle based on egoism and will of actions is superior to Kant's.

In the chapter 8, he discusses the problem of Formula of Humanity and Formula of Autonomy. In the beginning of this chapter, he starts criticizing FH by skirmish against concept of end and means for their being theological base. In Kant's proposition: "Man, and in general every rational being, exists as an end in himself," existing as an end in himself is a *contradictio in adjecto* because to exist as an end presupposes the will, but this essential relation necessarily excludes all *in itself*.[100] He even criticizes that Kant's base of worth in view of human reason is illogical when he says that beings avoid of reason are *things* and therefore should be treated merely as *means* that are not at the same time an *end*.[101]

Through this rugged path, Kant's FH reaches another supreme principle of morality, but already the reversal of worth took place in treating reason as the only source of distinguishing between an end and means. But FH is no other than the proposition: "Injure no one; on the contrary, help everyone as much as you can," and to this second moral formula the alleged duties to ourselves are dragged intentionally and awkwardly enough.[102] He furthered his objection that this FH works as indispensable deterrent force to keep the law in treating condemned criminal as a mean, not an end. So he argues that this FH cannot be the supreme moral principle because it has, on the other hand, the merit of containing a fine psychological moral *aperçu*, for it indicates *egoism* by an exceedingly characteristic sign, distinguishing the *opposite*.[103]

Against the third and last formula of autonomy of will (FA), Schopenhauer criticizes that it removes motive as well as interest when willing something out of a sense of duty; as the result it excludes the concrete base from consciousness or experience. He also disparages Kant's kingdom of ends set up from his formula of autonomy of will (FA) as being full of *rational beings in abstracto* without willing anything. In a word, he attacks FA as unreal and abstract concept which is derived from the conception of *dignity of man* but this one also rests on his *autonomy* and *law* of his own making. Kant defines *dignity* as "an unconditioned incomparable value",[104] but it is no more than hollow hyperbole as the *contradictio in adjecto*, because it doesn't include comparable estimation although value is the concept of comparison.

After this criticism he once again returns to his former conclusion that Kant's categorical imperative of pure practical reason has no concrete foundation coming from human consciousness or experience, rather it is a substitute for theological morals.[105] He briskly utters his final verdict against Kant's categorical imperative like this saying:

> "Our result, therefore, is that Kantian ethics, like all previous systems, is devoid of any sure foundation. As I showed at the very beginning in my examination of its *imperative form*, it is at bottom only an inversion and a disguise of theological morals, in formulas that are very abstract and were found apparently a priori. Such disguise must have been the more himself with it, and actually imagined he could establish, independent of all theology, and could base on pure knowledge a priori, the concepts of the *call of duty* and the *law* that obviously have a meaning only in theological morals."[106]

In this section, we have reviewed Schopenhauer's criticism against Kant's categorical imperative, but from next section we are going to review other scholar's criticism against Schopenhauer's moral philosophies in relation to Kant's categorical imperative.

(B) Critique Against Schopenhauer's Moral Philosophy

After severe charges against Kant's moral philosophy, especially in the perspectives of categorical imperative, Schopenhauer reveals his thinking with the conception *'compassion'* centered on his moral philosophy. In referring to his thinking, we cannot know other's suffering, so we cannot be any help to preventing or eliminating it, but if we consider it first of all independent of all other considerations, we can participate in their sufferings by our compassion in our everyday living, and all our well-being and happiness lies in this. He says further:

> "It is simply and solely this compassion that is the real basis of all *voluntary* justice and *genuine* loving kindness. Only insofar as an action has sprung from compassion does it have moral value; and every action resulting from any other motives has none. As soon as this compassion is aroused, the weal and woe of another are nearest to my heart in exactly the same way, although not always in the same degree, as otherwise only my own are. Hence the difference between him and me is now no longer absolute."
> 107)

Chapter 4: Morality

But against his idea of compassion as foundation of moral philosophy, many philosophers show such objections that Schopenhauer's moral philosophy has revealed many vulnerable parts. So in this purport we will review several philosophers' suggestions carefully and after that, we will ultimately decide which perspective of both is more justified and received as the genuine criterion of our moral philosophy.

In his paper, *Schopenhauer's Criticism of Kant's Theory of Ethics,* Tsanoff analyzes Schopenhauer's piercing criticism against Kant's moral philosophy, and negatively concludes that Schopenhauer does not fully understand Kant's moral philosophy, especially his categorical imperative. Initially Kant excludes 'experience' and human 'consciousness' as the foundation of moral philosophy for the reason that they cannot guarantee the supreme principle of morality because of their unclearness, changeableness, and even no absoluteness. It has no experiential or anthropological base because from the beginning Kant tries to establish moral philosophy on the supreme principle of *a priori* basis of 'pure practical reason'.[108] Secondly, Schopenhauer criticizes Kant's categorical imperative as having no ancestral foundation except theological origin. Schopenhauer thinks that Kant's moral philosophy based on categorical imperative is no more than the theological morality. He also finds that Schopenhauer finds Kant's categorical imperative itself to be only a paraphrase of the Golden Rule, of which his own maxim, *Neminem laede, immo omnes, quantum potes, juva,* is but the more adequately formulated statement.[109]

Tsanoff summarizes Schopenhauer's own theory of moral philosophy as the one emphasizing living humanity, not mere 'rational beings', so he psychologically analyzes that there are two main springs in human heart: Egoism and Malice. All vices come from these two sources, so to be moral means to cease selfish consideration. In this sense sympathy is the only base of morality because with it we want to stop woe of others and enhance other's weal. In order to prove this theory he appeals to human experience, and definitely concludes that *sympathy is thus seen to be the psychological basis of all morality.*[110]

But Tsanoff criticizes Schopenhauer against his theory of ethics focusing on sympathy and self-obliteration. He thinks that Schopenhauer's morality of sympathy is but a step on the road to salvation, but its real goal is self-effacement and its final result shall be racial self-annihilation.[111] This means that ultimately his moral philosophy leads to the extinction of all human beings; therefore Tsanoff agrees to Nietzsche's criticism against Schopenhauer in that such a moral philosophy leading to self-annihilation of human species cannot have any real meaning as the morality in the cold rational beings.

Tsanoff also points out that Schopenhauer misses the real spirit of Kant's 'imperative' ethics although he rightfully suggests that Kant's categorical imperative is too abstract in its so-called pure rational form to include the aspects of human experience and consciousness as the true basis of morality. He sharply expounds that although Schopenhauer shows the excellent analysis of Kant's categorical imperative as egoistic based on the theological absoluteness, but misses it's 'autonomous' character, so he propounds Kant's categorical imperative because its kinship to the reality is no other than the expression of man's own true self, in which he shares in the organic character of all experience.[112]

Finally he develops his own thought on the concept of sympathy which is the center of Schopenhauer's moral philosophy. He concedes sympathy as an important factor in the development of social consciousness and ethics, but it cannot be all of the moral life. In this purport he agrees to the egoism in the struggle of individual survival, and the narrow limited sense of duty, virtue, and happiness cannot reduce human beings into the dictatorship of the morality; rather realization of man's real self should be cooperated for the moral ideal world.

Paul Guyer's criticism against Schopenhauer is very similar to Tsanoff's, but he denies the serious difference between Schopenhauer's and Kant's moral philosophy in that the former thinks compassion arises from the pure theoretical reason by metaphysical insight into the unity of all beings, but the latter grasps pure practical reason as the source of respect to the moral feeling, and he supports Kant's is the more realistic theory on this point.[113] He suggests that in contrast to Schopenhauer's criticism against Kant, Kant does not reject compassion as an important conception of morality in his exposition of duty as leading to the first formulation of the categorical imperative.

Guyer says:

"So maybe he (Schopenhauer) just ignored Kant's recognition of 'love of human beings' and feelings of 'sympathy' in this work ....In the end, Kant as well as Schopenhauer recognizes a necessary role for compassion in moral motivation."[114]

But the fundamental difference between them is that to Schopenhauer the role of compassion in the morality is completely central and its main goal is the alleviation of other's suffering with considering reason not essential incentive for morality, while to Kant sympathy is necessary but not complete and sufficient incentive for morality with regarding reason as essential to the morality of humankind. In this context Schopenhauer sees compassion flowing from the metaphysical insight into the unity of beings based on pure theoretical reason, but Kant regards sympathy as the natural tendency of human beings but the one needed to be guided, corrected, and cultivated by reason.

Guyer points out that Schopenhauer objects to Kant's categorical imperative in the sense of deep-rooted egoism in human nature regardless of Kant's suggestion of its coming from pure practical reason, and secondly Schopenhauer criticizes that Kant's ethics based on duty is no more than theological one, especially from the Decalogue. These two points are almost the same as Tsanoff's, but Guyer analyzes both philosophers' distinction with more elaborate texture into his own views.

Guyer criticizes Schopenhauer against his dogmatic objection to Kant's claim that virtue emerges from 'the concept of duty and categorical imperative', in other words, from pure practical reason, and also criticizes Schopenhauer's argumentation that compassion is the highest moral incentive, and the only possible motivation for morality is the alleviation of other's suffering, and it comes from the pure theoretical reason.[115]

Irwin's criticism against Kant is sharper than Tsanoff's and Guyer's by analyzing Kant's and Schopenhauer's own moral philosophy very carefully and criticizing Schopenhauer's argumentation against Kant's categorical imperative very emphatically. In his voluminous book of *the Development of Ethics Vol. III*, Irwin says Kant suggests that moral imperatives depend on a justifying reason with no antecedent desire, but Schopenhauer argues that there is no such justifying reason; here Irwin criticizes that Schopenhauer misunderstands the role of commands and imperatives in Kant's account of moral philosophy with his assumption of justification and motivation, because it doesn't seem to fit either non-moral or moral reasons.[116]

Irwin also criticizes Schopenhauer against his objection to Kant's Formula of Universal Law for the reason that it is based on self-interest, and we have no duty, so we need not follow it. Irwin says that Kant's Formulas of Universal Law does not rest on self-interest; rather it rests on calculation about the unlikely counterfactual circumstances by which to judge his maxim according to the universal law. This does not mean all actions come from egoistic consideration in contrast to Schopenhauer's misconceived orientation without any self-interest from morality, which makes him misunderstand Kant's true intention of the Formula of Universal Law.

Irwin shows us very clearly how wrongly Schopenhauer conceives Kant's Formula of Humanity in mistreating subjective end as an objective one. But the Formula of Humanity, however, is not simply an attack on egoism, since it exposes an important moral error that is not confined to egoism. So Kant's demand for treatment of persons as ends extends further than Schopenhauer recognizes.[117]

As to the Formula of Autonomy, Schopenhauer negates Kant's suggestion that actions of morality are based on the responsibility of free will, because they come from the phenomenal level, not noumenal level; in fact noumenal reality is only one. Irwin criticizes Schopenhauer against this suggestion, for all determinations of free will come from the noumenal morality, and from one noumenal reality we cannot distinguish from different phenomenal realities, so he supports Kant's idea of Formula of Autonomy.

From this idea Irwin also criticizes Schopenhauer's emphasis on the 'compassion' as the central concept of morality, because by receiving Schopenhauer's idea we cannot presuppose that my phenomenal self and the other's phenomenal self manifest the same self.[118]

Finally, Irwin concludes that Schopenhauer's argument undermines morality unknowingly by charging Kant's idea of rationalistic morality and abstract categorical imperative and putting forward 'compassion' as the supreme principle of morality, which is the wrong metaphysical basis of morality although it is worth while agreeing to his sharp pointing out Kant's weaknesses in his absolutization of categorical imperative.

(C) Relation of Reason and Morality

After researching Kant's categorical imperative and Schopenhauer's moral philosophy very carefully, I come to reach the conclusion that Schopenhauer's criticism against Kant's categorical imperative is very unreasonable and dogmatic; it may be based on his misunderstanding of Kant's idea and the wrong metaphysical basis of 'compassion' as the moral motivation.

Schopenhauer's argumentation against Kant's categorical imperative is very simple: Kant's categorical imperative should be rejected as the moral principle because it is not empirical and has no concrete real substance in the conducts of man. But when analyzing his argument, I cannot but be struck by his lack of understanding of Kant's categorical imperative.

Schopenhauer is wrong in his negation of Kant's categorical imperative because it is just the thought processes, but it is not thought processes coming from the practical reason. Of course, it looks like some formality of moral law, but all laws have some formality regardless of their contents; therefore the law of morality may well have the formality. There can be no such a form without material once being thought in human intelligence, so Kant's categorical imperative has some formality as the moral law but surely in it there seem profound contents (materials) which can implicate all kinds of moral actions in human everyday living.

But the problem of Kant's categorical imperatives is that in his theory all moral laws have its origin in the pure reason although he states it comes from practical reason; here we must ponder seriously whether the first principle of morality comes from reason or not, but if human morality has some empirical base, his suggestion is right, but if it has its innate property not in reason but divine spirit, his idea should be very wrong, because in essence the morality should be above reason; in other word, the morality is not based on reason; rather it is essentially divine, and in this sense oriental thinking about the first principle of human morality has some advantages over western one in that they admit of divine originality in the human morality.

Next, Schopenhauer's suggestion that the law of morality must be empirical is seriously misconceived in the true essence of morality. If empirical actions can be judged by only empirical law of morals, they cannot be justified for their results because already the moral laws are relative, so they cannot be applied to all persons in all circumstances; this means that there is no absolute criterion of moral judgment. This case is referred to from Socrates' struggle against the Sophists who insisted that there should be no absolute criterion of morality because all morality of human beings is made from the well-being and convenience of man, so man is the measure of all things, which was said by Protagoras. Unlike them Socrates strongly believed that human morality has unchangeable and absolute foothold in the human soul, which comes from gods who are supposed to have lived in the eternal world. Although his saying cannot be proved in the speculative cognizance, we can guess that human morality is absolute

Chapter 4: Morality

beyond all mundane values beyond the mundane changeable properties.

In comparison of Socrates fighting against the relativity of morality, Kant's categorical imperative seems similar to Socrates, for we can know there can be absolute idea in the universe, but we are ignorant of it. Although Schopenhauer shows sharp insights to moral principles, Kant's categorical imperative is somewhat better reasonable than Schopenhauer's for our further research of essential moral philosophy although both arguments against a priori or a posteriori originality of morality seem futile, because the origin of human morality shall be divine.

In addition to Schopenhauer's criticism against Kant's categorical imperative in the cause of above two reasons of thought processes and no empirical foundation, I criticize Schopenhauer's charge against categorical imperative in that there will be no supreme principle of morality which comes from the pure practical reason. In my thinking there is surely supreme principle of morality, because without it morality cannot be possible, in other word, human morality comes from the unique nature of human beings, and it is divine spirit. Regardless of epistemological truth that all knowledge comes from human cognizance based on pure reason, all morality has the origin in our divine spirit on which our maxims of free will can be oriented toward the universal law of morality; in this sense Kant's strict idea of formality of categorical imperative has some portion of truth as the supreme principle of morality although not totally, because the ultimately supreme form can conclude all our moral actions, but Schopenhauer's peremptory negation of this rational formality means no receptacle with many contents; this is originally impossible.

As to the imperative form of categorical imperative, Schopenhauer criticizes Kant's categorical imperative for the reason that its imperative form *'du sollt (though shalt)'* comes from theological Decalogue, but this argumentation has no historical and documental base; rather it comes from the general imperative form of morality founded on divine spirit. Unlike Schopenhauer's suggestion of compassion as moral motivation, morality originates not from instinct but from inner imperative which can look into the hidden nature of order and necessity of the command of universal law of nature.

As regards to the moral motivation, Schopenhauer argues that all moral actions come from self-interest whether short or long perspectives on one's own calculation and our actions are by nature orienting toward conceiving others as our means, so the ultimate goal of morality is empting ourselves and regarding others as the same one as myself. This idea cannot be justified because our maxim must always match universal law of morality, so that whenever we act we should not conceive others as means but ends. This is the noblest principle of humanity (FH), then our morality should work toward the coexistence of all humans, but this does not mean that we are the one in our selves like Schopenhauer's argumentation. I cannot be you at all, and the concept 'we' does not mean that I and you are always one. The morality cannot go to the level of Schopenhauer's self-effacement, which is supposed to come from the oriental idea of Buddhism, in which self-forgetting and being united with the universe as the one unity are emphasized.

Schopenhauer's two concepts of compassion and self-forgetting shall not be the first principle of morality, still less Kant's categorical imperative is, because Kant's idea is in fact based on divine spirit; in other word he transfigured this principle into no less than reason-based categorical imperative. Schopenhauer sets his 'compassion' as the moral principle from which all his critiques against Kant results, but compassion is just emotional feeling for other's poor condition and it cannot be the supreme principle of morality because to every person, compassion cannot be the same; rather it is different from all varied circumstances. In this sense Schopenhauer's concept of 'compassion' is a kind of unprincipled subjective moral standard which cannot be justified at all.

And Schopenhauer's argument that our moral actions comes from the phenomenal reality cannot be justified, because they are based on only temporal and changeable situations, so all morality should be based on the noumenal reality, from which our phenomenal moral actions result. Although Schopenhauer praises Kant's transcendental idealism about space and time, his deviation from the noumenal principle of morality cannot be qualified as the supreme principle, for all the freedom of moral actions can be possible only on the noumenal free will which is no other than the Formula of Autonomy (FA); regarding this criticism I support Irwin's sharp criticism against Schopenhauer's perspectives on the autonomy of the free will.

Judging from above all criticisms against Schopenhauer's moral philosophy, Kant's categorical imperative has its own merits as the permanent moral standard and his five formulae of categorical imperative are good moral principles. Although Kant does not reveal the divine spirit as the foundation of his categorical imperatives, humankind should think much of and research morality more profoundly with them as the clue to human morality principle for the brilliant enhancement of human moral consciousness.

To this stage we have discussed the relation of reason and morality, and there we found that the origin of morality is not reason but divine spirit; in other word we can know and cognize the principle of our natural world and our inner heart not by our reason but by our spirit, which is supposed to have come transcendentally, not empirically from something unknown, whether it is God, the creator of human beings and all others in the universe, or ultimate beings which transcends us in all ways, or the universe itself, which is thought to have revolved automatically and endlessly without any purpose or aim; anyway the origin of our morality shall not be reason but divine spirit which is fundamental essence of our beings, for it can only function as the first principle of our whole beings in sensing, understanding, and reasoning something.

In all moral theories there has underlain something transcendental, which cannot be defined clearly; for example, the first principles of oriental morality shall be another explanation of this divine spirit; for example, Tien in Confucianism, Buddha in Buddhism, Tao in Taoism, and inner

Chapter 4: Morality 143

voice in Socrates are all another paraphrase of divine spirit, even categorical imperatives of Kant is another version of divine spirit; therefore all argumentation against the first principles of human morality in the history of philosophy has been proved useless without presupposing the existence of divine spirit on the base of morality.

In this sense the reason should be denied as the foundation of human morality without acknowledging the divine spirit, because human reason has been believed to have the logical function as the base of syllogism and the criterion of judgment in the scientific axiom, called the logical coherence of reason, and it has participated in the sustenance of human material life as the instrument of selfish protection and extension, labeled the instrumentality of reason. The only position in which reason can be designated as the base of morality may be the enlightenmentality of reason, which presumptuously proclaimed that it must lead men from the ignorance and illusion to disillusionment and illumination, but as we discussed in the previous chapter, it was also dismissed because of its inherent limitation and incapability, so that this should not claim its proper position in the human morality.

Of course, Schopenhauer's tough assertion of empirical foundation of human morality against Kant's imperative which is believed to have come from practical reason of which origin is pure reason, which has not empirical tint at all, affirmed its transcendentalism, but these two antipodal insistence on the origin of human morality shall be as much void as contention between rationalism and empiricism in the origin of our knowledge, because if the morality has the empirical base, it shall be transformed into relative principle, and shall not have the absolute validity as the moral principle, for all empirical principle shall be relative results however profound and elaborate system of self-evidence; secondly if the morality can be found in human reason, pure or practical, it shall also have no supreme universality of moral principle, because reason also has not proved as the ultimate validity however much it may be assured of its transcendental property in it, so that if reason is the only criterion of our moral principle, then we cannot be confident that we should follow its direction toward the universal well-being of mankind; therefore this is also another falsehood of major premise.

The morality of man has its supreme validity beyond all men, because if not, it would be effective on only some portions of men, not the whole, but its influence should be on whole men in humane boundaries; therefore the origin of morality which can satisfy these two premises cannot be found anywhere except the divine spirit, which is believed to have come from the absolute being and function as the supreme being in which all human organs and capability are operated according to the predestined code of our lives, therefore this divine spirit shall penetrate into all parts of our soul and body, and prescribe our actions according to already input code: conscience and inner consciousness of morality, which provides us with our maxims, moral or immoral, but whenever we act, we are imperceptibly conscious of the inner voice which can judge right or wrong against our actions, even our deep inner senses.

The origin of human morality cannot be justified in any empirical sources or doctrinal commandments or reasonable negotiation between the powers of good and evil; rather it is over the human boundaries, but it should not be matched like that mad Nieztsche's superman, because man cannot excel the boundary of human morality coming from divine spirit, which can be absolute as well as universal in its foundation and application to the actual lives.

To this stage we have discussed mainly the essence of morality in the perspectives of the first principle and the relation of reason and morality in view of its origin, but from next chapter we should research the relation of society and man in the development of morality.

Chapter 5: Society and Man

As we have discussed in the previous chapter, the morality of man is concerned about society, especially its security; this means that the purpose of morality should be focusing on the protection of the society; in other word individual man cannot act against the society, because one pervert man will endanger the security of the most men in the society as in the recent cases of international terrorism which gloomily threatens the security of the society which is damaged by the terrorism, so that in the cause of protection of the society individuals should endure all kinds of unfair treatment and be watched over, and all human rights can be denied in some urgent situation, so individuals cannot put one's own rights over social protection. This is the usual phenomena in almost all countries of the world, whether advanced or developed or underdeveloped ones.

When looking through the history of mankind, there has never been such an ideal society as human rights and dignity have been kept and protected perfectly; rather society has been thought much of while negating the individual human rights, so that we cannot think that individual man has the proper status in the society in the clamorous slogan of total well-being and happiness. In this purport society has not been the cradle of man; rather it has been the tool of oppression and exploitation; then here we may ask why only man should have the morality for the society and why the society should not have the morality for the individual man although some countries are practicing the welfare policies based on democratic socialism.

Chapter 5: Society and Man

The history of mankind can be defined as the battle field of ideological self-extension for the cause of strengthening the society, not for individual man, so that men have been in fact slaves of the society in the shackles of all kinds of ideology, laws and statutes, taxes, forces, and even morality, which have never been asked or questioned of their validity in the taciturn enforcement and absolute obedience; therefore man has been very feeble and powerless being before the society, particularly violent powers of the state.

In any sense, without any reasonable measures, man could not be good terms with the society, which might have the unilateral power against individuals in the hands of very limited elites who exert power over all regions of the society, and men should follow their tyrannical leadership without asking such doubtful execution of the powers of the state, so that in fact men in the society have been enslaved this or that way; therefore we should consider the way of prohibiting the evil man in the summit of the power ladder from executing their unlimited power over the weak and powerless men of the society. In order to fulfill this purpose, first of all we should criticize the past wrong theories of society and man, in which man has been the sacrifices for the totality only, and society has been regarded as more valuable than individual man, while almost all such theories tried to clarify the essence of justice in the society, but they have had the tendency of emphasizing one part; for example, some scholars focused on the totality of the society in the cause of social welfare, although this perspectives were oriented toward the enhancement of the living standard of the poor and weak, the results were so much contrary to the general expectation, because the social system which some pioneers had visualized in their mind turned out terrible after reformation at last. This results from the inevitable contradiction of the concepts of society and man, both of which have dialectic properties in each one, so that the harmony in both shall be a kind of miracle; in other word, the organic function of the society cannot correspond to the individual man from their innate difference and uniqueness. But regardless of this inevitable limitation we must look for the desirable principle of social philosophy for the harmony of society and man.

I. Critique of Ideology

(A) Concept of Society

The question of the relation of society and man has been very controversial because of its dialectical characteristics and ambiguity of the constituent principle of both realities. First of all, the definition of society is not clear, because we generally think that society is the group of people who has the definite object of living together under the coherent principle, while this definition is to some degree overlapped with the concept of community because community has almost the same one as we see the definition in the dictionary.com: *a social group of any size whose members reside in a specific locality, share government, and often have a common cultural and historical*

Chapter 5: Society and Man

heritage.[119] This concept cannot be distinguished easily from the one of community except that it has more spatial meaning than the one of society, but here we are not going to analyze the difference between both definitions, rather we will criticize the presently hegemonic theories of society which have influenced so strongly that our idea of society cannot easily evade from those ideas: Those are functionalism, liberal or Enlightenment theory, and conflict theory. But these three theories have had their own inherent contradictions; e.g., firstly, functionalism cannot be established if it compares society to the human body as a biological function in contrast to Luhmann's theory of autopoietic social systems, for society is basically different from the human body and it is just the reflexive thought of human organs as comparing to biological being.

Secondly, Liberal and Enlightenment thinkers overlooked the limitation and destructive nature of human reason over religious or hereditary authority, and social progress. Unlike their optimistic view of liberal theory, free individuals will not progress by their power of free reason over time and reach the ideal goal of free and equalitarian society in which all members would be able to be prosperous, enjoy their own happiness and self-realization, and the society will be better and better over time passage by the accumulation of human knowledge and wisdom. But in contrast to their rosy perspectives, human society has been degrading and worsening due to the wrong application of reasonable thought to their own self profit by the serious misuse of human reason in the instrumental aspects, so that if it does not connotate liberally demolishing aspects of society by the reason over traditional authority and conflicting friction between human and society, society cannot stand to itself as an independent being.

Thirdly, conflict theory looks the society in the most pessimistic view in that they conceive the society has been the field of human struggle because of the inherent conflict between different interest groups, so that society cannot stand itself in the static stability; rather it continually changes because of underlying inevitable conflicts in all human relations, distribution of material values in the people, and fighting against each other for occupying ruling position. So conflict theory emphasizes division rather than consensus of theory: for Marxists theorists the society is no other than the struggle between divided classes for occupying more material possessions, and for gender conflict theorists and LGBT, society is divided by gender and weak women and sexual minorities who have been always taken advantage of by men or sexual majorities. Other conflict theorists like anti-racist and anti-imperialist have also seen society in the perspectives of human conflict. But their unbalanced view against social consensus or good human properties have blocked human society from progressing and advancing toward the noble ideal society.

But all these three theories of society have struggled against their own contradictions and inevitable own limitations without being considerate of other position of theories; in other word these three theories have their own advantages and weaknesses, so that they have revealed their vulnerable points reluctantly, and must be revised in consideration of the truthful concept of society.

Here we can know that the critique of society should be the one against all the hegemonic political ideologies like capitalism, neoliberalism, socialism, and communism, for they have influenced us so strongly that we cannot evade from their effects, good or bad; even we ourselves have been defined according to their complicated and sometimes untruthful self-rationalization although we have never criticized and attacked their own unreasonableness and cruelly demolishing humanity whether intended or not, so that main political ideologies of human society have been already idols of our weak people and timid community, in which they have adjusted themselves to the ideologies however much doubtful and conflicting they may be in sane sense of our normal brain.

(B) Critique of Main Ideology

Firstly, capitalism has been proud of its prosperous productivity and luxurious material glory, and whoever tries to get the best profits of their labor and production can be supposed to be surely prosperous if they are clever in dealing with huge trade or selling their own merchandise, but without deceiving market and even maneuvering market trade, their growing appetite for money cannot be fulfilled however much they have poured their power, energy, and material possessions in their enterprise because in some time the market would be disappear with devouring all appetites by its own limited size and capacity; in other word, unlimited competition to acquire as much market as possible should lead all the concerned to the destruction finally; therefore uncontrolled struggle against each other for money would make them fall into the pit of self-demolishment. However, the capitalism seems very virtuous when all the concerned have kept their position not with the covetous self-interest but with the good Samaritan humanity to live together as much equally as possible and share their properties with other poor and weak people in the society, if not, it would finally result in the monster of fascism and imperialism.

Against neoliberalism we cannot criticize them too much, for they have focused on forfeiting as much money as possible from all the parts of the world whether they collapse or not, they aim at making money beyond the boundaries of the countries and their capitals have squeezed the poor countries, and they move here and there to hunt many bonanzas, but the biggest problem is that they willfully overlook the humanity and commonwealth of the whole world and support the most powerful imperialistic camps with no consideration of the terrible results of the destruction of the humankind; even they have dreamed of the elegant lives of their own leagues without the troublesome poor and weak by scheming their own paradise somewhere on the earth; then we cannot help looking their true identity and deep-rooted satanic nature of cruelty.

Socialism has been misunderstood and misused by many ideal activists who have had humane face and a saint of a heart for the commonwealth of the most people in the society, but what is laughable about the misuse of the term is that

Chapter 5: Society and Man 153

socialism has been in fact interested in the individual well-being of the community while they always have emphasized the importance of the society and the total equality of all the members of the society, but in contrast to their original intention, socialism has not guaranteed human individual welfare and self-realization, for in human society there has never been completely ideal society of guaranteeing individual happiness, but we have been seriously forced to respect the totality and autocratic leadership; then we should consider how much socialism has negatively influenced us and how wrong it has led humankind into this chaotic situation; of course somebody would argue against me in that in western Europe socialistic society has paved the carpet of commonwealth of all the people in the society by levying more and more taxes from the wealthy persons, which they have felt too burdensome, so that these governments have been really socialistic in their executing social policies; then here we must ask them whether all the common people have been really blessed and finding their lives well worth sustaining. Surely in these countries socialism has tried too often realizing the ideal of socialism: commonwealth of all the people and guaranteeing the equal condition of their lives in the communities. But we have witnessed their groaning over degrading their morality and quality of their normal lives, and this overshadows on us the ominous future of their societies.

Communism has been praised by too many radical idealists although it has its inevitable contradiction: first of all, its presupposition of the equal society in which individuals work to their capabilities and be distributed to their needs, and this is no more than a fraud or empty slogan which would not be fulfilled, because resources are limited to human appetites which seem limitless, in other word, human wishes for the good and desirable life in the world in which material resources have been always limited against all human needs. Perhaps Karl Marx visualized the ideal society in his wrongly imagination of primitive communities where all materials are shared by the members, but from the beginning there has been no possibility of such an ideal communism society in the human history except the very short period of early Christian communities just after the Jesus resurrection and ascension to heaven; therefore in any sense the communism society would not have been possible from the start of human history, for the right of possession could not have been alienated to anyone at all because of its necessary characteristics of self-sustenance.

Secondly, communism has negated the individuality of all the beings in the universe, especially of men, for in the world there has no same or equal men; all are different in the figures, characteristics, and capabilities; therefore communism has misplaced the equality as their basic slogan to guarantee the well-being of all the proletariats in the society; their argumentation is as such forfeits the wealth of the bourgeois and monopoly in the few hands of the ruling classes represented by the professional trained radical elites; this fact can be proved in the past history of many countries which had been revolutionized by the communist parties. The equality of all members in the community is no other than the illusionary

Chapter 5: Society and Man

ideal and by nature impossible daydreaming of insane or imbalanced mind.

Thirdly, their way of revolution by violence shall not guarantee the establishment of the ideal society for which they have poured out their power, energy, and effort superhumanly, for almost the results of their revolution has been the seizure of hegemony in political, economical, and cultural execution of the powers of the country into the very limited group of elites who had been chosen and trained to carry out the revolution, so that the terrible tragedies of human massacre by the communism parties in the cause of the founding of ideally equal society whose regimes always go toward the abolition of bourgeois classes; even they decimated more than thirty million people in USSR by Stalin, more than twenty millions in the People's Republic of China during the period of the Cultural Revolution, and more than two millions in Cambodia by Pol Pot, etc. If you admire such dictators of communist regimes and expect to see the ideal society by massacre of huge numbers of people except you, in that case you shall be assured rest, but the point is that you would be included in the one of the people killed unconditionally and mercilessly without any legal procedures and just judgment by the conscientious judge, but would be maltreated, tortured, and forfeited your divine life, then you would realize the essentiality of the communism based on the hatred and fighting and massacre by the very limited devilish numbers of professional revolutionists.

In addition to above serious problems of communism, we can find a lot of fundamental contradiction and irrationality in it, especially the planned economy system by the state seems very awkward and unreasonable in the standard of economic principles, in which almost numberless economic units have worked mutually and operated on their individual economic interests, and the economy system has been too complex and intermingled with other parts of the country to be controlled by the state at all; therefore as we see in the People's Republic of China, the state already gave up communistic economy system once being merged into the international capitalism system. Here we can know that the state can supervise the free markets run by the people, but she cannot control them tyrannically in the bureaucratic ruling system by the communistic method.

But in consideration of limited space, we are now going to concentrating on criticizing Marx's most important thoughts although his theory seems to be so much complicated that we cannot criticize it easily. I will here try to review Marx's analysis of merchandise value theory carefully, because it is really the essence of his whole system of communism.

(C) Critique of Marx's Merchandise Value Theory

Karl Marx has been known the initiator of Scientific Socialism and wrote an immortal masterpiece, *Capital*, in which he analyzes concretely capitalistic production system in the capitalistic society and reveals its operation rule and innate contradiction of the capitalism. For this purpose he starts his analysis of the secrets of the 'commodity' which has been produced by human labor but leaves laborer immediately on

Chapter 5: Society and Man   157

being completed. The reason he starts his analysis of the capitalism from the commodity is that in capitalistic society the wealth exists as "an immense accumulation of commodities", and its unit being a single commodity[120], so in any sense a commodity is a kind of incarnation of human life by self realization of the laborer.

So from the chapter 1 of *Capital* Volume 1, we shall analyze his idea of the commodity on the base of assignment questions by the method of hermeneutics, and for this purpose we will pursue this theme by the order of ① the commodity as the fundamental unit of capitalist society ② the relation between use-value, exchange value, and value ③ the relation between concrete and abstract labor ④ the dialectical contradictions in Marx's identification in treatment of the commodity form ⑤ the culmination of those contradictions in the "fetishism of commodities", and ⑥ conclusion.

Although this task is not easy matter to fulfill, it will be so much helpful to understand Marxist philosophy and after this job we are surely going to have some useful tool with which to launch on understanding another theory of proletariat revolution, his unfinished work on this earth.

① The Commodity as the Fundamental Unit of Capitalist Society

In human history, there has been a lot of form of the wealth. In primitive times people might have regarded as their wealth needed raw materials for their sustenance like fish, animals, or plants, etc., But in feudal society, the land was the most important riches and one's level of the wealth was judged by the degree of their occupation of the estate, so all kinds of struggles and war resulted from possessing the land. But after industrial revolution, all economic system began to focus on the occupation of the production system, so from arising of Bourgeoisie class, the capitalism deeply penetrated into the social system, and the concept of wealth has been changed from the land to the commodity.

In the capitalist mode of production the criterion of the riches lies on the commodity, so from the production and selling of commodities the wealth can be accumulated, and it became the most important characteristics of the capitalism. Furthermore all our everyday living can be possible by using and spending some forms of commodities which are made for others' usage, so without proper providing commodities for other people's using, human life could not be possible. What is more important in the capitalistic society is that all values, corporeal or non corporeal can be materialized in the context of human history as some form of commodities, so it is called the fundamental unit of the society. From this background, Marx began to analyze the commodity as the key to criticize capitalistic society, and it is very reasonable and insightful research to look into the contradictions of the capitalistic society, and from the point we can proceed to remedy the system and put forward the desirable economic system to secure all people's well being.

Chapter 5: Society and Man

Next we are going to analyze the values of a commodity which are materialized in the historical and social context.

② The Relation between Use Value, Exchange Value, and Value

When a commodity is produced out from raw materials in the capitalist mode of production, it should have some value from which it is regarded as a satisfying item of human needs. A commodity has two elements of value: use value and exchange value. Use value is the utility of a thing which makes the item something useful, but it is not a thing of air but physical properties of the commodity, and it has no existence apart from that commodity.[121] The utility of each commodity forms its use value, and this is fulfilled when using or spending the thing in reality, so use value means the utility which is revealed when a commodity is concretely used in practical life.

However, all commodities have exchange value in addition to use value at the same time, so a commodity is conceived as a thing in which use value and exchange value exist together. Then, exchange value is presented as the quantitative relation and as the proportion in which use values of one sort are exchanged for those of another sort, and this relation is constantly changing with time and place.[122]

Here Marx explains exchange value in more detail with examples of real commodities like wheat, blacking, silk, or gold. He shows the relation of their different values like one quarter of wheat has the same value of x blacking, y silk, z gold, etc., and this means that they have their own exchange values. So exchange value is the exchangeable one by which one commodity is exchanged with another one by some definite rate of the same value.

Marx suggests that what determines the exchange value of a commodity is the value of a commodity, so he identifies the concept of exchange value as the one of value.

③ The Relation between Concrete and Abstract Labor

Marx says that the value of a commodity is materialized by the amount of labor time in the normal social surroundings of production and the productiveness of labor, so if labor time is constant, the value of a commodity can be changed by the productiveness of labor, which is determined by various circumstances. So the value of a commodity, therefore, varies directly as the quantity, and inversely as the productiveness, of the labor incorporated in it.[123]

After analyzing a commodity in the perspectives of value, Marx points out that in a commodity are mixed two values of use value and exchange value, and he finds out that if looking at a commodity in the labor there are also twofold nature: concrete labor and abstract labor. Marx emphasizes the importance of this duality of labor in understanding economics and attributes the clarification of it to his credit.

First of all he expounds that 'the concrete useful labor' is the labor whose utility is represented by the value in use of its product, or which manifests itself by making its product a use

Chapter 5: Society and Man

value.[124] This is interpreted that concrete useful labor produces use value in a commodity, so in the use value of a commodity there should be contained useful labor, i.e., productive activity of a definite kind and aim. In other word, different use values of different commodities come from the concrete useful labors, for example, a coat and linen are different commodities with different use value which are produced by different labors of tailoring and weaving. So 'the concrete useful labor' is the labor which produces use value of individual commodity.

In contrast to this concrete labor, the abstract labor is the one which abstracts use value from all the labor and identify all productive activities as the expenditure of human labor power. If explaining this abstract labor by the examples of tailoring coat and weaving linen, these two labors are the same in that they are no more than the expenditure of general human labor power because they use human brain, muscles, and nerves although they are different special labors. The reason a coat and linen has exchange value by the definite rate is that in the two commodities is contained identical human labor power. So abstract labor means the general human labor power which produces (exchange) value of a commodity.

Here we can summarize both concepts in the perspectives of human labor power: the concrete labor is the one which produces use value in the commodity with definite means and goal, but the abstract labor is identified as the general human labor power which produces value of commodity.

Now we stop analyzing concrete and abstract labor here and are going to review the dialectical contradictions in Marx's identification in treatment of the commodity form although this may seem the most difficult part of understanding his idea about commodity.

④ The Dialectical Contradictions in Marx's Identification in Treatment of the Commodity Form

Marx thinks that in the commodity there exist innate several conflicts and contradictions, which can be the innate problem of capitalistic economy. The first contradiction of the commodity is the conflict between use value and (exchange) value. This means that once being produced, a commodity should have some useful value to the purchaser but in fact it is automatically led to the mysterious world of commodity, which has some post in the network of the commodity world which are separate from the real world, so it is already transferred to the generalized value; i.e., the exchange value of the commodity. Here the use value of the commodity loses his original property and assumes totally different characteristics. This comes from the inevitable properties of human labor. Originally human labor is put into the coarse raw materials to produce some item which is visualized in human mind, and it is produced from human labor power which uses brain, nerves, muscles, and hands. But after being produced, the item assumes the characteristics of commodity and the concrete labor begins to assume the abstract power together with the transformation of use value into exchange value of the commodity, therefore the dialectical contradiction between use value and exchange value

Chapter 5: Society and Man 163

cannot be evaded from its deep rooted dialectical mixture of the value system of the commodity.

The second contradiction of the commodity is that in the commodity private labor should be represented as the social labor simultaneously with production. This contradiction comes from the social characteristics of the commodity, because when one produces some items from raw materials for his private purpose, they cannot be conceived as the commodities, but if such raw materials are produced as the commodities, they will immediately assumes the social properties and come to have some relation with the commodity world in the social context. Here we can find the conflicts of the commodity as to its socialization from the private region. When looking into this phenomenon in the social economic system, the capitalistic society seems possible on only the commodity trade, so without the socialized commodity it could not sustain itself; for example, if one day one major oil company were to proclaim that they would not sell any oil commodity like gasoline to private car owners, there might take place enormous calamities in the society, so any commodity may well have its original connection to the society however private labor produce such items, they would be surely socialized commodity without considering private labor of laborers, so their private labor would be also transformed into social labor and the private item should be the socialized commodity, and laborer cannot do anything for his own produced item.

The third contradiction of the commodity is that concrete useful labor is counted as only abstract general labor. What this means is that when laborer works to produce some items, he pours his concrete useful labor power to them, but when some commodities are produced out from the production activities, the commodities lose their own original aspects and suddenly moves to the socially generalized items, so the concrete useful labor also is transformed into the abstract generalized labor in the appearance of the commodities. This contradiction is deeply relevant to the second one, that private labor is directly represented as the social labor in the commodity, and both are matching the presupposition of the socialized properties of the commodity. In fact labor power produces privately some items, but these are issued out publicly to the world with totally different aspects of the commodities, so they are not related to the concrete useful labor but only appeals to the public. In this stage laborer should give up his own incarnation of labor power by exchanging his labor with another commodity, the same value of money.

The fourth contradiction of the commodity is the conflict between the personification of the commodity and the commercialization of the person. This means that once produced, the commodity presents itself as the alive being like person, so it shows off and exercises its labor power around it and come to have relation with other commodities in the context of the social network. But the laborer is isolated himself after seeing the materialization of his abstractness in the commodity. Here the laborer feels alienated from the commodity and falls to the passivity in which nothing can be obtained despite his pouring labor power into the commodity.

Chapter 5: Society and Man   165

So as a commodity it becomes alive like a person and prides itself of and enters into the relation with the other commodities in the social networks, but laborer loses his personal positivity and falls into passive ossified being not to act as a subject in the relation with the commodities which are surrounding himself.

All these contradictions of the commodity are believed to be based deeply into the property of the dialectical movement of the labor and commodity, so human beings cannot control its natural tendency and usually stand passively without any positive response to the operation of the commodity. Marx's identification of these contradictions which are deep rooted in the dialectical nature of commodity and labor is so much sharp as to influence our desirable orientation of socio-economic system in the problematic capitalist society.

In this chapter we have analyzed Marx's identification of the dialectical contradictions of the commodity, but in next chapter we will see the culmination of these contradictions in the fetishism of commodities.

⑤ The Culmination of Those Contradictions in the "Fetishism of Commodities"

According to Marx, the contradictions of commodities have been culminated in the fetishism of commodities. Then, what is fetishism of commodities? Marx says that when labor production assumes the form of commodities, especially money form, it looks like having independent power and acts like an alive being. Marx says:

> "In that world the productions of the human brain appear as independent beings endowed with life, and entering into relation both with one another and the human race. So it is in the world of commodities with the products of men's hands. This I call the Fetishism which attaches itself to the products of labor, so soon as they are produced as commodities, and which is therefore inseparable from the production of commodities."[125]

Marx thinks that the mystical character of commodities does not come from its use value; rather it comes from the functions of human organism, which is the expenditure of human brain, nerves, muscles, etc., and human labor assumes social form regardless of its difference of the quantity and quality in any situation. Easily speaking, fetishism of the commodity comes from human nature with identifying one's own product as incarnation of labor power. So Marx says that a commodity is therefore a mysterious thing, simply because in it the social character of men's labor appears to them an objective character stamped upon the product of that labor.[126]

If explaining Fetishism more, we can say that once produced, commodities acts like independent beings, in other word, they seem to have separate value to be exchanged with other commodities. From this fact the human relation as producers is hidden and the personification of commodities appears on the scene like wholly independent alive things. This is fetishistic character of commodities.

Then, how are contradictions of commodities culminated in the Fetishism of commodities? Originally the contradictions of the commodity comes from the conflict between use value and (exchange) value, the representation of private labor as social labor, the transformation of concrete useful labor to abstract general labor, and the personification of the commodity and the commercialization of the person. And when we consider these contradictions of commodities seriously, we come to know these all contradictions are culminated in the fetishism of commodities by the more careful analysis of the characteristics of the fetishism.

First of all, fetishism of commodities means the absolutization of value of commodities rather than human labor. In Fetishism of commodities, commodities themselves are already regarded as holders of values themselves, so use value is easily neglected in it. And commodities can exert their power as holders of exchange values without considering their original use value, so here there occurs the culmination of contradiction of the commodity in the fetishism of commodities.

Secondly in the fetishism of commodities we can see the inevitable socialization of private labor, because in it we can see only socialized aspects of commodities, i.e., in it the property of private labor was already forgotten entirely and only commodities with social value come upon us.

Thirdly in the fetishism of commodities we can see the ultimate abstractness of concrete labor in the socioeconomic system; in this order all concrete useful labor has been equated as only one goal: the profit, so commodities just act as the only functional agents to guarantee it, and from this fact we can witness the culmination of flagrant contradictions of commodities.

All these contradictions are seriously contributive to the culmination of expediting the human alienation by the conspicuous personification of commodities and the striking commercialization of persons. All these contradictions of commodities are functioning synchronically in the society once labeled as commodity, and human beings have been shunned as subjects of their production, but fallen to the objects of commodities; from this tragedy all our universal and moralistic value of human beings has been forgotten, and the elated glaring ghost of Fetishism of commodities, the Mammon has been the idol of our contemporary civilization.

⑥ Conclusion

Nowadays commodities have already occupied the noble post of humanity and act like the master of all people, so today may be called 'the era of dictatorship of commodities'. But if interpreting this phenomenon, we can know that there lies the devilish spirit of Fetishism of commodities, and noble humanity which should respect labor as the utmost valuable one already disappeared, so in all the fields of our society Fetishism of commodities perverts all other values and forces us to worship another god, which is another externalization of human idolatry, the worship of Mammon.

Chapter 5: Society and Man 169

In this sense, Marx's achievement of analyzing commodities is really superb, so without this idea about the commodities we could not penetrate into the contradictions of capitalistic society. Although his analysis of use value and exchange value is somewhat lack of more profound clarification of essential nature of commodities' value system, we can get at the exponential importance of value in commodities. His analysis of concrete labor and abstract labor is also very sharp, but it is also problematic to explain the intercourse of the two labors in the production of commodities.

His pride in expounding deep-rooted contradictions of commodities may well have the good ground, because with his application of dialectical movement to the operation of commodities in the capitalist mode of production, he could lift himself to the immortal post of Initiator of the Scientific Socialism. From his excellent thoughts on the Fetishism of commodities, we cannot but be overpowered before the horrible secret of commodities in our society; rather it comes upon us as the Revelation which augurs the upcoming destruction of human civilization.

Although to this stage we feel lack of more deep analysis and radical research, the completion of this task shall be another possibility to start better inventive critical thoughts by which to enhance the life conditions and social well-being for all the members of the society, so that we had better stop discussing Marx's merchandise value theory here and go toward the main theme of this book: Human Sovereignty.

II. Human Sovereignty

What is human sovereignty? On what ground should we base our sovereignty according to the rule of unchangeable truth and divine humanity? Is there certain criterion of such unclear concept? Or is it just the illusionary dream in which we are just trying to enhance human conditions of ideal living?

As to these questions we are going to answer them on the base of truth, and progress toward the five main foundations of human sovereignty: spiritual life, seeking for truth, economical independence, political wisdom, and philanthropic share.

The word 'sovereignty' generally means 'having supreme power or authority as an independent monarch' [127], so human sovereignty means 'having supreme power or authority as a man', and from now on we are going to use the meaning of the word when man can apply his independent supreme power to deciding his own destiny to the best option by his own right and power. The reason I chose this term is that firstly, for describing human supremacy we are the owners of our own destiny and choosing our way of living in the perspectives of divine human rights, and secondly we are the children of God, who has created man according to his image.[128]

And this is not an unclear concept from which we misunderstand all connotations about human own right and capability to decide his own way of life; rather it has been merged into the concept of humanity, knowingly or unknowingly. And there is definite criterion among such seeming criteria when we apply it to the practical living, that is, the ultimate judge of human sovereignty is God's Word, which has been revealed to us through general revelation, the natural world, or special revelation, Bible, whether we recognize it or not; therefore the concept is not just the illusionary dream in which we are just trying to enhance human conditions of ideal living, but when we lead our lives according to the absolute value of it, we will be able to witness our well-being and prosperity in all our ways of living.

This concept is superbly important to our establishment of ideal new society instead of wrong and radical ideology like capitalism, neoliberalism, socialism, and communism, etc., so that it is now more and more urgent to clarify the concept more deeply and widely than ever. In this perspective we are going to expound the five foundations and requirements for human sovereignty; spiritual life, seeking for truth, economical independence, political wisdom, and philanthropic share.

(A) Spiritual Life

Essentially men seeks for the absolute being whether perceiving God or not, so that without the knowledge about him, we feel uneasy and stressed unknowingly. This fact is known from the Augustine's famous saying, "Thou hast made us for Thyself, O Lord, and the heart of man is restless until it finds its rest in Thee."[129] Why do not we find peace of mind without God in our heart? The reason is that the basic constituent of man is spirit beyond our body and soul as I said in the beginning part of this book. What is more striking is that almost everyone in the world leads each life in the principle of religion, and the number of people in the world who believe in any kind of religion in 2012 is more than 7167 million according to Wikipedia.[130] This shocking demographics shows us clearly that man cannot live without some beliefs in the ultimate being although some atheists are confident that they can live without God, but then they also believe in another absolute being, "Nothingness"

In the world, there have been a lot of people who trained themselves spiritually in the deep mountains or some lonely and quiet place; they pray to ultimate being in this or that way by murmuring some unknown words or spell; they read or memorize their own scriptures diligently; they practice deep breathing regularly and meditation; even they go into the waters for so long time, and even burn themselves for the sacrifice to their gods. All these practices have been done with some faith in the ultimate beings, so that we cannot deny the existence of religious influence on them at all in contrast to the Marx's slander against religion when he proclaimed that religion is the opiate of the masses.[131]

But the problem is whether or not people believe in true deity and do their right religious practices in their living; if we believe in false gods or wrong religion, then they would lead us into the worst situation like being fallen into the heresies or devilish powers to being forfeited chaste of one's spirit or physical body and possessions. Here we can say that leading a spiritual life should be founded on the true and right religion which identity has been proved good and profitable to human mind in social level.

Here I can illustrate one example of the importance of leading spiritual life; it is the case of Free Masonry, for they require all applicants to have faith in their deity regardless of its kind and characteristics, so that if an applicant confesses his faith in 'for example' Buddhism, it is OK! How much absurd should it be if their purpose should be the true fellowships and enhancement of the community, because people with different faith would not be harmonious with each other easily and ultimately they would be locked in the serious feud, jealousy, and fighting against one another.

Here we shall reach the conclusion that we must choose true and right religion based on the truth, love, and salvation of our spirit, and according to its instruction we should lead a spiritual life so that we may fulfill our human sovereignty.

(B) Seeking for Truth

In Korean saying, "The ignorant act bravely."[132] This is a kind of paradox because the ignorant cannot act easily in the state of unknowing something, but have many cases of misbehaving or making mistakes; in this sense our lives should be based on the truth, which has been conceived right, good, and one since the ancient times.

The reason the truth is right, good, and one is that they are the essential properties of the truth; which means that first of all, the truth can be differentiated from the wrong facts or properties, because the truth itself is justified in the fact only, and it can guarantee the righteous way of being; secondly the truth should be good, which means that it is always useful or profitable to the practical sides of being, so that it fits man's reason in the intelligence and knowledge as well as practicality; thirdly the truth is always one, which means that it cannot be divided or diversified but should be always unified in the essence, so that its result always should be the same although its appearances shall be diverse.

If one's life is not based on the truth and led by the falsehood or hypocrisy, its way shall result in the undesirable or even destructive because life shall be deviated from the beginning through the course to the end, degrading and falling into the worst result, so that for human sovereignty our life should be founded on the truth. For the purpose we should seek for the truth in every way of life, which can be supposed to have been realized in every academic discipline, but especially we should find the truth of life in the philosophy like Socrates who had devoted himself to the philosophy and awoken young men to let them ask themselves to know themselves when he was declared the wisest man in the world by the divine oracle in the Delphi temple when he used to say, "As for me, all I know is that I know nothing."[133]

In fact, the self-awareness of ignorance is the starting point from which we can seek for the truth of life whenever we come to be empty, and this should be the continual procession in pursuit of eternal truth in our whole lives.

(C) Economic Independence

The great Chinese thinker Mencius once said that "only when the people had a steady livelihood would they have a steady heart."134) This meaning is that men must get the continual income to live stably, so that without proper job which guarantees the substantial income, man would be wanderer without any established location of livelihood. In order to live decently, we must get the job by which our livelihood is guaranteed, whether we are blue collar or white collar workers or professional men. This fact has been too much emphasized on communists in the side of blue collar workers named proletariats who are supposed to lack continually proper income to sustain them and their family members, but this is not limited to them but to all the workers who must gain proper amount of money to live by.

But in society many people cannot find good job to live by, because the number of jobs is limited, but the one of job seekers is too many to be distributed to them equally, then rest of the job seekers who lost the opportunities of job finding should continue to lead unstable and tragic life in the sense of self-abandonment and depression. In this sense, in order to keep human sovereignty, individual man in the state should be guaranteed his livelihood in being supplied with shelter, clothing, foods, and means of cultural life on condition that he is willing to work faithfully and has the capability to pour his energy and power to the designated job.

We should not be poor Socrates who had not produced any money for sustaining himself, his wife, and his sons in the cause of awakening Athenians to realize their ignorance, for however noble his philosophic life might be, his incapability of economic independence would kept him from overcoming worldly obstacles resulted from all financial matters, but in this case we are inclined to be depraved and further fallen into the self destruction.

If society cannot help individuals find the proper job and make them earn money to live by, then they would be endangered in adjusting themselves to the society as independent men, and would be the vulnerable factors of social unrest, so that this would hinder men from keeping human sovereignty in everyday living, because it is deeply rooted not in the material abundance but in the balanced well-being of soul and body with the substantial income guaranteed.

(D) Political Wisdom

Man cannot evade political life however much he may try to do it, because before his birth, his living condition has been already circumscribed, and this cannot be changed until he leaves his present situation. Therefore we should face calmy present political situation whether it fits our tastes or not, especially we shall not be satisfied with the ideology of my country, but overthrowing this political circumstances might be almost impossible as powerless individuals; this can be likened as a man before the huge mountain like Mt. Everest. What I

Chapter 5: Society and Man

mean is not that we should give up all challenges against the present wrong political system, especially terrible dictatorships but we should be more and more wise in enhancing our countries.

If you are in the state of ultra right or left fascism, I dare to advise you to defy them not in the temporal or irascible passion but with your utmost wisdom which will protect you, your families, and your friends. The reason of my saying this is that revolution will surely need substantial passage of time with the serious corruption of present ruling parties' and adamant unity of resistance camps with the wise and strategic leader groups who will devote themselves to the noble cause of human sovereignty.

If we are in the state of liberal democratic society, we are easy to be ruled by the power of a handful of tycoons who have unimaginable amounts of money, and in this state legal election process would be formally summary course from which their hegemony would be continual while their mammonish power lasts in the society. In this state we would have no other means to elect only one party between just two or several parties which have bustlingly propagated that their party only will protect the rights of the voters and enhance the living standard of theirs by their superb platforms and policies, but we would feel upset and even disappointed after they leaves the terrible results of their regimes behind.

In fact, in the capitalistic society the election process cannot fulfill rosy future unlike their brilliant promise, because the regimes would fill the storage of huge capitalists with the finally unimaginable profits, and the pockets of the normal persons would continue to be empty as usual in the deplorable regret and resentment against the regimes, therefore we voters should be always awake with not believing in present regimes and future prospective parties whether they may blow trumpets to the highest level, because we would be once again deceived by them helplessly for their inevitable nature of self-interest, self-esteem, and self-sustenance by too much spending voters' bloody taxes and labors.

Therefore man with human sovereignty should be more and more wise in electing his leaders and public servants in an election, not by paying attention to his own interests but to the commonwealth of the country as well as people's individualistic profits. For this purpose man should speculate on the correct method of politics and establishment of social and individual welfare with sharp criticizing all political ideologies and all parties' platforms and policies in view of the human sovereignty.

(E) Philanthropic Share

When we have come to this stage, we should focus our lives on living together with our contemporaries regardless of their racial, national, or sexual origins, because as I am the child of God with his image proper, so they are the same one. This is the divine solemn commandment of God. If my life is only for mine, its value is limited to me, but when we look around we shall face each other with the same human

Chapter 5: Society and Man

sovereignty; therefore living harmoniously with neighbors means the true reason of our well-being and others' ones.

Then, we should share our goodness with our neighbors, especially the poor and the weak, because they are not others but reflexive we with the same nobleness and sovereignty although their present situation is such as poor, weak, sick, and even dying. This is not suitable to Kant's categorical imperative by which our human morality is exerted in the hard form of universality, but this is proper to the divine people with mutual understanding, affection, and devotion.

To reach this step, we need to share our possessions and talents with them, because all of them will not guarantee our ultimate salvation and well-being despite its abundance and brilliance; rather when they are shared with other people, we cannot but feel the utmost blessings from our deep inner parts as well as outer ones. So if you do not feel any shame when you eat luxury dinner with your family members only by overlooking the eyes of the poor out of the window who have felt hunger and thirst for almost three days, then your heart are already ossified with no compassion and mercy for them, and even came to the ultimate level of just enjoying your luxury and talents for your self-interest and profit; therefore at this moment your human sovereignty was already broken off to the level of brutal and cursed demons.

Sharing your own possessions and talents with the poor and weak always leads you into the glorious pleasure of living together with your contemporaries and divine good beings in your heart as well as your spirit, so that we had better start the life of sharing ours with others, and the sooner the better. Here our noble philanthropic humanity will have been established, and human sovereignty would also appear as the supreme power of taking lead its way of progress toward the ideal society.

To this stage we have reviewed constituents of human sovereignty in the practice of our daily living, but these perspectives are really personal level as individuals will exert the power of human sovereignty. But however much we may focus on individual lives based on human sovereignty, it would not guarantee our own happiness and well-being; rather we would confront the social contradictions and conflicts in the midst of individual upgrade, then we should visualize the ideal society or state in which all the individuals will have their own human sovereignty. Accordingly we are about to turn our attention to the institution of the ideal state.

III. New State as the Institution of Human Sovereignty

Humankind has been continually progressed in the aspects of material prosperity with the profound application of science and technology to everyday living, so that outwardly our living conditions seem to have been advanced outstandingly, but inwardly humankind has come to the stage of gruesome and inhumane fall with no peace and rest in his mind; this is very paradoxical because men surely achieved material prosperity but have been degraded spiritually, and cannot expect any more blissful life; we don't know the correct reason of present unrest and anxiety, but what is clear is that present society based on the inherited ideologies cannot be validated or justified any longer because of their horrible results at this stage, therefore society should be reformed according to the epoch-making project of new humans. Here we can presuppose that new society will be possible only by the institution of new state based on human sovereignty. From now on we are going to search for the route to the new state with five constituents made up for human sovereignty

(A) Freedom

To this date men have insisted on the achievement of an ideal states to guarantee human freedom by their all good measures and policies; especially western civilized countries have asserted their extensive application of human freedom in all fields of state policies, so that their people have come to the final stage of human well-being in which human freedom can be enjoyed heartily.

But unlike their assertion the inner states of their people have been seriously perilous because of their spiritual depletion, and what is worst is that they have been forfeited their freedom more and more in the cause of protecting their security against terrorists. Therefore it really matters how we can keep our freedom in the pessimistic state of our contemporary days.

Freedom should not be limited in any situation, because without it we cannot sustain ourselves. In other word, freedom is like an air of our spirit, without which we cannot breathe spiritually and just be suppressed in being suffocated to death. But what I connotate here by the term of freedom is not traditional concept of being free from any bondage; rather it is the unlimited expansion of one's own self-realization in the society, so that the state must not only prohibit all negative restriction and control against all individuals but also actively guarantee them their own self-realization in the society.

Nevertheless freedom does not mean self-indulgence or free violation of state law, rules, and regulations; rather it is unlimited expanse of one's own self-realization within the self-control by which to abide them, for human freedom could not be achieved without the strong support and encouragement of the state and consensus of all the people in the state. In this sense the principle of freedom should be the cornerstone of the new state to go toward human sovereignty.

But this freedom can be obtained in the social system in which justice is overall established as the cornerstone of social lives. So from next section we are going to discuss the social justice in the perspectives of human rights toward human sovereignty.

(B) Justice

Justice never means the balance between only classes, because it should be applied to all individuals equally whether rich or poor, strong or weak, wise or foolish. Generally constitutional state can exert justice more effectively than the autocratic one, for autocrats cannot judge all cases with the balance of law because of his emotional favoritism. It is the same as the ruling classes have unique power to control state affairs with usual persons' having no possibility to intervene in them; in other word unilateral execution of powers over state affairs would result in the final corruption and destruction of the state.

Nevertheless the principle of check and balance in all state branches cannot secure the overall justice in all individuals, since the living condition of the poor by birth cannot match the one of the rich by birth, and they will not grasp the opportunity to rise in the upper ladder of society as ruling classes. Also their different standards of living could not be equalled at all however much the state may pour out all resources to make them equal to each other. Then where does justice exist in the state affairs? If it does not mean the equality of living conditions, what makes us feel justice in the state affairs?

Here we must newly define justice as the conditional institution of granting equal opportunity of self-realization to every individual without any forfeiture or limitation of its freedom by the state, because with the strong intervention of the state all individuals can expect their self-realization in their life on condition that they do not give up their hope of it, in which man can only feel peace, rest, and blessing permanently.

But granting equal opportunity of self-realization to every individual would be fulfilled under the social circumstances in which human rights should be guaranteed to all individuals if they abide by law, rules, and regulations which has been agreed upon by the free constitutional will of all the people. Then, here we need some more thoughts about the human rights, so from now on we are going to review the concepts of several representative scholars of human rights.

① Concepts of Human Rights

Thomas Pogge's concept of human rights is in a word an institutional understanding of them; what this means is that human rights are grasped in the context of social system politically, economically, and culturally, and he thinks current notion of human rights has evolved out of earlier notions of natural law and natural rights.[135] According to him, from this process of evolution the concept of human rights has been deepened, but he emphasizes the close connection of human rights to the moral concern. This is expressed in the equality of human individuals in the matter of human rights. His view is easily ascertained in his saying:

> "All and only human persons have human rights and the special moral status associated therewith. The expression also suggests that human beings are equal in this regard. This view can be analyzed into two components. First: All human beings have exactly the same human rights. And second: The moral significance of human rights and human-rights violations does not

vary with whose human rights are at stake; as far as human rights are concerned, all human beings matter equally."[136]

Next, he suggests that modern notion of human rights be the official disrespect of human rights-that is, the violation of human rights. This means that human-rights postulates are addressed, in the first instance at least, to those who occupy positions of authority within a society (or other comparable social systems.)[137] And he lists the government as the official human rights violation agents and in order to evade this violation of human rights by the government, people should be the ultimate guardian on which their fulfillment crucially depends.[138]

His next important concept of human rights is an interactional understanding. This means that human rights should match the corresponding duties. In other word, human rights are always presupposing the moral duties. He says:

> "On my understanding, too, human rights (conceptually) entail moral duties-but these are not corresponding duties in any simple way.[139]

In conclusion, he makes his idea of the institutional understanding of human rights by positing that human beings have common basic needs and that in one's society all should enjoy the basic needs by the criterion of the same morality in the threats of official violation of human rights.

Maurice Cranston's concept of human rights is in some sense very similar to Pogge's, because he also defines human rights as a form of moral right, which is basically different from the other moral rights in the sense that it should be universally applicable to all people at any situation. In describing the concept of human rights, he sharply separates it from economical and social perspectives. In his thinking, the example of the vacation with salary should be universal human rights but in reality it cannot be applied to all countries for the reason of their own economical, social, and cultural situations.

In contrast to the above two authors' concept of human rights, Kwasi Wiredu's one of human rights in view of Akan's position is very different from above both of them. According to him, Akan tribes are very humanistic in dealing with human rights. He analyzes their concepts of human rights in the perspectives of two different angles: the first is the personal level and the second is the social level. As regards to the personal level of human rights, he says that Akan people think it natural that all the newly born have the innate rights to be nursed and educated by the community to which they belong; even they have right to be educated for the matter of sexual reproduction, and when they grow up to adults, they can have the better important rights for their sustenance, that is, occupying lots of land.

As regards to their social rights, they have the right of being guaranteed franchise in any political organization to self-government including the right of electing leaders of the society and deciding governmental policies. They also have the right of freedom of thoughts and expression in all matters, political, religious, and metaphysical, the rights of everybody of

Chapter 5: Society and Man

trial before punishment, the right of a person to remain at any locality or to leave, and so on.[140]

From these democratic and modernized human rights, we can summarize their principle of human rights in the perspectives of God, human, and society; therefore their interpretation of human rights are closely connected to the divine creator, maternal lineage of ancestors, and the society as the fields of supporting their lives in the standard of equality and respect.

As regards to the Buddhist's concepts of human rights, they seem to have no concrete definition because of the innate religious limitation centered on the transcendent spiritual region which has been totally different from the conventional western concepts of human rights. From this position Damien Keown tries to prove the existence of Buddhist's concepts of human rights. He cited Rev. Vajiragnana's thinking that Dharma (the principle of beings in the universe) determines mutual duties between human relations like husbands and wives, kings and subjects, teachers and students. In this sense human rights comes from respect and protecting others' rights first.

But Kenneth Inada bases Buddhist's concepts of human rights on the human nature as the ultimate source of human rights and it means the interrelatedness of humans[141]; that is, all humans are by nature connected to each other deeply, so they have the same destiny as humankind, so we cannot deny or neglect other people's rights as we cannot be denied or neglected our human rights, so this is defined as the doctrine of dependent-origination.[142]

In contrast to Kenneth Inada, professor Perera suggests Buddhist's alternative concepts of human rights by the human dignity. He cites Jean Jaques Rousseau's and Kantian concepts of autonomy, that is, self-governance as the foundation of human rights in Buddhism. This means human rights comes from reason and autonomy from which men can build up themselves into society to protecting themselves.[143]

Damien Keown concludes his thinking about human rights in reviewing all concepts of human rights from several Buddhist scholars; so he concludes that Buddhist's concepts of human rights are based on post-mortem nirvana, which means the ultimate possibility of self-realization which means in their sense being Buddha from the perspectives of Dharma, which is revealed in the knowledge of oneself and moral value as the interrelated beings in the society.[144]

To this stage, we have reviewed concepts of human rights from several authors' writings, but from now on we are going to review the norms of universal human rights so as to validate and set up the criterion and the universality of human rights.

② Norms of Universal Human Rights

Are there norms of universal human rights? As to this question, I will say in somewhat emphatic tone, "Yes, we have been inherited them from our traditional teachings of religion and great thinkers, but they have been deeply hidden to contemporary days in the dark illusion of human culture and selfishness of all people's struggle against all people as Hobbes's saying.

In my opinion Poggie suggests two norms of the universal human rights: Firstly, all human beings have exactly the same human rights (equality), and secondly, the moral matter of abiding or violating human rights is equally applicable to all humans. (morality) These two norms of universal human rights seem to demarcate the universality of human rights clearly in the very narrow sense of moral importance, but in the wider sense of universal human rights coming from human nature, that is, the natural law, but this is too much slanted to grasp the norms of universal human rights. Rather he focuses his analysis of universal human rights on their violation by the authorities, especially governmental ones. So his orientation toward universal human rights has slanted slightly negative analysis of their violations.

Cranston's norms of universal human rights are focusing on social and economic ones, so the traditional human rights such as the rights to life, liberty, and a fair trial are treated as political and civil rights. He lists social and economical rights like unemployment insurance, old-age pensions, medical services, and holidays with pay as universal human rights.[145]

Wiredu's analysis of Akan society shows us similar modernized norms of universal human rights in the perspectives of the equality of mutual respect and well-being from sustenance help-this is really like contemporary welfare state of western countries. But in my opinion their universality cannot match the welfare state of contemporary days because of their sticking to the conventional ways of tribal living, especially in the adjudication and punishment of the dead persons and the unconditional distribution of land to their members of the tribes, but their generosity of freedom of thought and expression can make me conclude carefully that there are conspicuous norms of universal human rights in the Akan society.

From Damien Keown's suggestion about the Buddhist's concepts of human rights, we can easily grasp the norms of universal human rights; in other word, Buddhism starts their thinking in the universality of human beings, that is, the existential truth of universal beings in the universe, therefore, in the Dharma they can set up the norms of universal human rights. Their first emphasis on this is all beings in the universe have innate possibility to be Buddha, so universal human rights starts from this absoluteness of human dignity as prospective Buddha. Their second emphasis on this is the equality of all beings which are interconnected to each other deeply, so their destinies are also on the same foundation. The norms of universal human rights are deeply based on this thinking, so we must respect others like ourselves and must not hurt or damage others in any case. Keown's analysis somewhat lacks oriental profound views because of the tendency to analyze Buddhism in the western way of thinking and logic.

To this stage, I reviewed the norms of universal human rights from the several authors' suggestions or argumentations but in the next section, I am going to show my position about the concepts of human rights and the norms of universal human rights.

③ Human Rights Toward Human Sovereignty

Human rights are the innate and inalienable rights of men who were born on this earth, so they cannot be seized or forfeited or yielded to other person because of their absolute properties. Firstly, the most important human right may be the right to live, which means we humans have the nature to like living and dislike death. In this sense the right to live should be guaranteed and protected against any governmental or authoritative or powerful private threats. We humans are born to live although death awaits us from the distant future.

Secondly, another important human right is to live freely, which means that we have the tendency to follow our own natural instincts, understanding and reason, so we like to live freely, not to live in bandages. In this sense freedom is very important human rights, without which we cannot be expected to realize our selves desirably.

Thirdly, the equality of human rights is too important to deny, for without equality of our dignity we cannot be satisfied with the repeated occurring disparity and terrible worsening conditions of our living; we have seen that terrible inequality of living conditions have led us the way to the revolution of which the results have not been always propitious to the poor and weak people.

Fourthly, we want to live happily, but this is not fulfilled only with our efforts and struggles because the society which is the foundation of our living has not always been supportable to us or profitable to our living; rather sometimes power of society forced us to devote ourselves to some goal or ideology sacrificially, but the results have not been always what we have expected, so the rights to pursue our happiness in our living should be obtained from the suppressive or unfavorable society.

These human rights must have the norms of universality, without which the society would fall to the heinous war field of the survival of the fittest as Darwin's saying. From the highest religion like Christianity and Buddhism we can find the most desirable norms of universal human rights; the former uplifts universal human rights to the God's children and the latter to the absoluteness of the self in the universe. The Universal Declaration of Human Rights by the UN can be the cornerstone of universal human rights, but we must know it is just the manifesto which items should be fulfilled presently or in some day.

Of course universal human rights presuppose the absolute fulfillment of each individual's self-realization, but to this date this noble ideal has not been totally completed from the deep-rooted human wicked personalities, so that the way to guaranteeing those universal human rights to each person lies far away; in any sense it might be impossible to reach the goal, but we must go forward to reach the apex of human sovereignty from which to satisfy all the people on this earth for their full self-realization.

If we summarize the above discussions about the human rights in two words, they would be 'equality' and 'autonomy'; then these are paraphrased as following: All men have the equal human rights on condition that they decide on their destiny by their autonomous will and the state must respect their human sovereignties with the least intervention in their lives for their happiness and self-realizations.

On this foundation we are going to search for the way to establish genuine democratic society in this contradictory world.

(C) Democracy

There have been all kinds of democracy in human history and political system as well, and there has never been so much misunderstanding as the concept of democracy, because all ideologies have suggested that theirs have fulfilled the true denotation of democracy, so there have been direct democracy, representative democracy, people's democracy, liberal democracy, social democracy, industrial democracy, etc. But in view of original meaning of democracy, it means *government of the people, by the people, for the people*[146] as Lincoln said in the Gettysburg address.

Of course, the power of democratic society has been believed to be in the hands of a few bourgeois elites whose interests have never been corresponding to the general people, but the merits of recurring election processes have kept them from exerting omnipotent power in the state affairs. Nowadays they may well say that liberal democracy has been called the most advanced political system in the history of humankind however much conflicting views there have been against it.

The most progressive system of political system is in fact direct democracy, under which all individuals in the local communities participate in the political affairs and exert their own commissioned power over it. But in western countries instead of it, elite politics has been influenced substantially by Plato whose mentor was Socrates, who tacitly infiltrate the danger of democracy and encourage to young men in Athens government by wise philosophers, who can devote themselves only to the state affairs by impartial and unselfish judgment and leadership, however, in contrast to his good intention it contributed to the establishment of all kinds of fascism government whether ultra right or left wing.

The new state seeking for the human sovereignty should stand in the liberal democracy with devising and enhancing it anyway, for so as to guarantee freedom, justice, and social welfare to people, it can only be workable to progress toward the noble human sovereignty.

But in order to oil the liberal democracy well, the state must educate individuals as thoroughly and profoundly as possible, because the foundation of it is really on its constituent people. If the people are just snobbish and selfish, the state would be perilous and easy to collapse as in the case of Athens in Socratic days because of its shortage of wisdom and ruling morality. In this sense liberal democracy cannot sustain itself if the state is not equipped with brilliant intellectual power of the majority of the state; rather it would be fallen to the

Chapter 5: Society and Man

mobocracy against the general will and commonwealth of the society.

Nextly the state must make most of the people prosper in their economic lives by enhancing the standard of the economic morality of the society and granting equal opportunities of upgrading their status to all the people if they industriously continue to work and make great effort in their economic lives. Here the state should try to distribute the national wealth to as many people and as much as possible by ingenious measures and philanthropic policies for the individual well-being of her members; what is more important is that the state should never give up the lower credit citizens because of their financial matter like business failure or bankruptcy, for if the state can only protect the prosperous and high credited persons, then the society would be their own league of exploitation and suppression against the weak and poor, so that the vitality and enterprising circumstances of the state would disappear and finally it would fall to the worst form of democracy: plutocracy; in other word, without the genuine comparative economic equality of opportunities, the society would be endangered in the dictatorship of oligarchy. Then here we need to discuss the way of granting economic equality of opportunity to all people by the method of desirable social welfare.

(D) Social Welfare

Although there has been a saying that even the state cannot save the poor[147], only the government can save the poor in the limited range of governmental budget. Since the beginning of the social welfare government in the occidental world in the 18th century, the aim of social welfare has been expressed from the famous expression, 'from cradle to the grave'[148], and this slogan has been the target of all social welfare state coherently despite its serious defection. But in the liberal democracy state it has always been objected to by the rich and power groups because of the undesirable effects on the financial stability and final bankruptcy of national budgets; therefore in any sense the social welfare state seems to be very dangerous in total perspectives of the state. But if the state does not exert the proper power over the urgent needs matter in the poor people, where can it find its reason of existence?

Nowadays it has been generally doubted that only one percent rich people of the world have harvested most of the worldly wealth and the poor have been more and more impoverished. Of course this might be the terrible aspects of merciless neoliberalism mixed with immoral and brutal capitalism; nevertheless new state also should focus on the establishment of effective social welfare system by mobilizing state wealth and distributing it properly to stabilize financial crisis of the poor people, and in other side encouraging enterprises to create added value greatly with creative innovation and high-skilled invention by least intervention and regulation of free markets.

This idea can be espoused by the fact that the government cannot be only the subject of spending expenditure of the state, rather it must be the subject of productivity and invention as a control tower of all the enterprises in the state; what this means is that the government of the state must be the acting subject of establishing, supporting, and expanding grand public project by which to share the fruits with her people. In this sense the new state should be the subject of unlimited responsibility of making money for her people and social welfare for them.

This would prevent social revolution from taking place in the cause of solving the poverty matter in the public, and the society would be progressed strikingly by the best productivity and effective distributing system based on the idea of human sovereignty although it looks very contradictory to one who favors totalitarian system and pursues radical reformation and speedy effectiveness in solving poverty matters in the public.

In conclusion, the best social welfare system would be possible only by the total mobilizing of national wealth with the supportive and innovating control of all enterprises in the state and granting jobs to all applicants by operating central big data system to employ them in the national level, and this means that without the outstanding influx of national wealth, the social welfare system would be impossible.

(E) Peace

The purpose of the state should be securing peace for the people and evading international conflicts. This should be the ultimate goal of the state which pursuits human sovereignty. But as we have witnessed from ancient times to the contemporary days, people have been suffered from all kinds of violence, invasion, and forfeiture by the strong states through terrible wars, and it seems the same as having been never changed; therefore imperialism and fascism still remains with a different masks, so that most of the world countries have tried to strengthen their military powers by purchasing the innovative high-tech weapons for mass massacre, and military competition among world powers has been worsened and worsened to this date.

The peace of the new state would be obtained by first of all the voluntary unity of the people against foreign invaders, and secondly being equipped with the best military weapon system, and thirdly strong domestic soldiers with high-spirit and good morale. But the most powerful measures against all invasions would be the total ultrahigh-tech defense system by the new state in which even nuclear attack could be checked in the beginning step and abolished before landing and exploding on its territories, and any invaders would be defeated critically with being damaged irrevocably, so that any enemy should be afraid of the terrible result of the invasion.

Peace without restraint power against enemies cannot be peace at all, because in any case the enemy can demolish our peace with deadly weapons like nuclear bomb or ICBM, therefore having the nuclear restraint power against any enemies has been more important than anything else. If it is impossible to have nuclear defense system on its own, the new state should be affiliated into the nuclear protection system of group affiliation like NATO; therefore in any sense, the most effective way to evade wars is the universal solidarity of the peace-loving countries whose noble destination has been the world peace ultimately. If not, any possible nuclear war would happen and the state would be demolished to a hell of a level.

Therefore new state in pursuit of human sovereignty must continually develop and advance the total ultrahigh-tech defense system in order not to be invaded or attacked by any traditional or nuclear weapons. This way only leads people to be holistically safe and allow them to enjoy their self-realization and glorify God through their mission on the Earth.

However, besides foreign invasion, in contemporary days the problem of peace against terrorism has been also another imminent threat to all world citizens whether right or left wing countries. But when looking into the deep-rooted cause of it, we cannot but be struck by the fact that all terrors have come from the serious hatred against the religious and political cleavage in the sects, so that it cannot be evaded at this stage with the normal preventive allopathic measures like anti-immigrant system.

Evil comes out of evil; this means that by the violent and suppressive method we cannot block the terrorists of the world, because men is by nature wicked and without the proper education and training full of love, men cannot escape from the camps of evil. In this purport, the education for loving others as well as myself should be launched as soon as possible from the beginning of a toddler to the end of one's life; if not, men cannot escape from the shackles of the evil powers, for our daily living teems with a lot of land mines under our feet, so that we cannot evade hating, resenting, and murdering others physically or spiritually. In this position we cannot secure the peace of our own as well as the society, for we are destined to be born and died in the midst of sins, then we should launch on a wholly new state which seeks for human sovereignty by instructing people for loving others as well as themselves.

But what is best to preventive terrors is that people must think much of the value of humanity rather than the one of money, fame, or power, so that the society would be always full of love and mutual understanding and magnanimity in every field of life.

Of course strict laws, rules, and regulations are required to the peace of the state, but what is more important is that the stern administration of them should be necessary for keeping society peaceful. Although some deviation from the normality can give some people relax and comfort to their mind and it more often than not affords creative and innovative spirit to our mind, the adamant abiding by laws must be forced to all citizens in the state without any exception and consideration of their social status, classes, and degree of education or wealth, so that this constitutionalism can only pave the way to holistic peace of the society.

In addition to these security matters like wars and terrorisms, there has been always the security problem of all the possible accidents from our daily living: fire, traffic accidents, building collapse, violence, injury, abduction, murder, medical accidents, suicide, etc. All these accidents would damage our lives so seriously that we cannot evade them easily in the personal level; then the state must be responsible for these security matters and start the proper measures immediately from educating the public officials to all people about the imminency and importance of the security against all kinds of accidents from our everyday living. So the route to the peaceful life of the state is above all establishing the consciousness of security in all the people of the state; what I means is that every individual should care about one's own security in every field of life; in another word, the total perfect security system of the state can be obtained by the higher level of security consciousness in the whole population, but the public officials must always take care of the citizens by utmost care and awakening alertness against all kinds of negligence, mistake, misbehavior, and despair. If not, our personal security cannot be guaranteed and man-made calamities would happen at any time unexpectedly and we would be endangered against the life and death matter in the terribly frustrating and desperate and inevitable situation.

The peace problem has been the most difficult and recondite matter during the history of mankind, and to this date there has never been absolutely peaceful state in the world, and we humankind have lived in the midst of all kinds of dangers, threats, and sufferings while at every moment of life enjoying such a trivial happiness as loving our own families and friends and tasting delicious foods and good wines, sometimes traveling. But without the stable peace of the state, individuals cannot live peacefully at all, but without the stable peace of individuals the state cannot sustain itself as well, then their dialectic characteristics of unity will have to be more deeply harmonious and non-conflicting, rather it should be always one affecting each other inevitably as the common destiny, so that the research for solving the conflicts between the individuals and the state should be launched immediately for the permanent peace of the world; the sooner the better.

ANNOTATIONS & BIBLIOGRAPHY

Chapter 1

1) Marx, Karl. (1875), *The Critique of Gotha Program, Part I.*

Chapter 2

2) Cassirer, Earnest. *An Essay On Man*, New Haven: Yale University Press, 1976, p. 25-26.
3) NIV. Genesis, 1: 27.
4) NIV. Genesis 2:7.
5) Kant Immanuel. *Critique of Pure Reason*, trans. Guyer, P. and Wood, A. W. New York: Cambridge University Press, 2008, p. 99.
6) Armstrong M. D. *A Materialist Theory of the Mind*, New York: Routeledge, 1968, p. 1.
7) Ibid., p. xi.
8) Ibid., p. 1.
9) Ibid., p. 1.
10) Ibid., p. 2.
11) Ibid., p. 2.
12) Ibid., p. 6-9.
13) Ibid., p. 10.
14) Ibid., p. 11.
15) Paul, Thagard. "Cognitive Science." in *The Stanford Encyclopedia of Philosophy* (Fall 2008), ed. Edward N. Zalta.
16) http://en.wikipedia.org/wiki/Cognitive_science.
17) http://en.wikipedia.org/wiki/Cognitive_science.
18) Sloman, Aalon. "The Mind as a Control system." in *Philosophy and Cognitive Science*, ed. Hookway, C. & Peterson, D. New York: Cambridge University Press, 1983, p. 69.
19) Ibid., p. 74.
20) Ibid., p. 75.
21) Ibid., p. 76.
22) Ibid., p. 78.

Chapter 3

23) Kant Immanuel. *Critique of Pure Reason*, trans. Guyer P. and Wood W. A. New York: Cambridge University Press, 2008, p. 387.
24) Hense, Elisabeth. & Maas, Frans. ed. *Towards a Theory of*

Spirituality, Walpole: Peeters, 2011, 29.
25) Plato, *The Dialogues of Plato,* trans. Jowett, B. New York: Boni & Liveright, 1927, pp. 374-379, p. 388.
This part is cited and translated from my M.A. dissertation of Yonsei University, 2005, p. 3.
26) Aristotle. *On the Soul,* trans. Smith, J. A. New York: Random House, 1941, pp. 559-562, 587-588, p. 598.
This part is cited and translated from my M.A. dissertation of Yonsei University, 2005, pp. 3-4.
27) Augustin. *De Trinity,* Cambridge: Cambridge University Press, 1967, ch. 10, 16.
28) Aquinas, Thomas. *Summa Theolgie,* New York: McGraw-Hill Book Company, 1964, p. 237-249, also see, Trigg, R., *Ideas of Human Nature,* Oxford: Basil Blackwell, 1988, p. 45-48.
29) Descartes, Rene. *Discourse on Method and Meditations,* Indianapolis: Bobbs-Merrill Company, 1960, p. 24.
30) Ibid., 132-133, 139-140.
31) Locke, John. *Essay on Human Understanding Vol. I,* Oxford: Clarendon Press, 1894, pp. 121-122.
32) Locke, Johna. *Essay on Human Understanding Vol. II,* Oxford: Clarendon Press, 1894, pp. 387-388, 390-392, 399.
33) Ibid., p. 404.
34) Ibid., pp. 86-91.
35) Ibid., p. 93.
36) Hume, David. *On Human Nature and Understanding,* New York: Collier Books, 1962, p. 236.
37) Kant Immanuel. *Kritik der reinen Vernunft,* Hamburg: Felix Meiner, 1956, B xvi.
38) Ibid., B 25.
39) Ibid., A 405.
40) Ibid., A VII.
41) Ibid., A 395.
42) Ibid., B 427.
43) Hegel, Georg W. F. *Phänomenologie des Gesites,* Hamburg: Felix Meiner, 1980, S. 132.
From this paragraph to the first one of p. 47. they were adapted and translated from my M.A. dissertation of Yonsei University, 'A Research on Max Horkheimer's Critique of Reason', 2005, pp. 7-9.
44) Ibid., S. 133.
45) Ibid., S. 134.
46) Ibid., S. 192.
47) Ibid., S. 215.
48) Hegel, Georg W. F. *Grundlinien der Philosophie des Rechts,* Hamburg: Felix Meiner, 1956, S. 11.

49) Han, Sang A. *A Research on Horkeimer's Critique of Reason*, Seoul: Yonsei Unversity, 2005, pp. 7-10.
50) Horkheimer Max. *Critical Theory*, trans. Matthew J., New York: Herder and Herder, 1972, p. 202.
51) Ibid., p. 204.
52) Ibid., p. 242.
53) This part is adapted and translated from my M.A. dissertation of Yonsei University, '*A Research on Horkheimer's Critique of Reason*', 2005, pp. 10-11.
54) Ibid. pp. 11-12.
55) Ibid., pp. 12-13.
56) Han Sang Y. *A Research on Horkeimer's Critique of Reason*, Seoul: Yonsei Unversity, M.A. Dissertation, 2005, p. 1.
57) Ibid., p. 1.
58) Ibid., pp. 43-44.

Chapter 4

59) "*Archived copy*". Archived from the original on 5 April 2011. Retrieved 1 April 2011.
60) Aristotle. *Nicomachean Ethics*, tr. Irwin T. Indianapolis: Hackett Publishing Company, 1999, Chap. 7, p. 8.
61) Ibid., p. 9.
62) Ibid., pp. 15-16.
63) Ibid., p. 42.
64) NIV, Matthew 22:37, 39.
65) NIV, Galatians 5: 19-21.
66) Sartre, Jean P. *Existentialism is a Humanism* trans. Carol Macomber, ed. John Kulka, New Haven: Yale Univ. Press, 2007, p.vii.
67) Nietzsche, Friedlich. *Thus Spoke Zarathustra*, tr. R.Z. Hollingdale. London: Penguin Books Ltd., 1969. p.41.
68) Sartre Jean P. *Existentialism Is a Humanism*, trans. Carol Macomber. ed. John Kulka, New Haven: Yale Univ. Press, 2007, p. 14.
69) Camus, Albert, *Second Letter to a German Friend*, December 1943.
70) Kant, Immanuel. *Groundwork for the Metaphysics of Morals*, trans. Thomas K. Abbott. Ontario: Broadview Press, 2005, pp.70-72
71) Ibid. pp. 72-73.
72) Ibid. p. 74.
73) Ibid. p. 80.
74) Ibid. p. 81.
75) Kant, Immanuel. *Groundwork for the Metaphysics of Morals*, trans. Thomas K. Abbott. Ontario: Broadview Press, 2005, p. 88.
76) Ibid., p. 86.

77) Ibid., p. 87.
78) Ibid., p. 89.
79) Ibid., p. 90.
80) Ibid. p. 96.
81) Larry Blum's Lecture Handout (Spring 2015, UMB),
    FORMULATIONS OF THE CATEGORICAL IMPERATIVE
82) Kant Immanuel. *Groundwork for the Metaphysics of Morals*,
    trans. Thomas K. Abbott, Ontario: Broadview Press, 2005, p. 95.
83) Schopenhauer, Arthur. *On the Basis of Morality*, trans. E. F. J.
    Payne, Indianapolis: Hackett Publishing Company, 1995. p. 48.
84) Ibid., p. 57.
85) Ibid. p. 95.
86) Ibid., pp. 67-8.
87) Ibid., p. 74.
88) Ibid., p. 76.
89) Ibid., p. 74.
90) Ibid., p. 75.
91) Ibid., p. 76.
92) Ibid., p. 77.
93) Ibid., p. 77.
94) Ibid., p. 89.
95) Ibid., p. 89.
96) Ibid., p. 91.
97) Ibid., p. 92.
98) Ibid., p. 92.
99) Ibid., p. 92.
100) Ibid., p. 95.
101) Ibid., p. 95.
102) Ibid., p. 97.
103) Ibid., pp. 97, 99.
104) Ibid., p. 101.
105) Ibid., p. 103.
106) Ibid., p. 103.
107) Ibid., p. 144.
108) Tsanoff, Randoslave A. *Schopenhauer's Criticism of Kant's Theory
     of Ethics*, The Philosophical Review, Vol. 19, No. 5 (Sep., 1910),
     p. 514,
109) Ibid., p. 513,
110) Ibid., p. 522.
111) Ibid., p. 530.
112) Ibid., p. 533.
113) Guyer, Paul. *Schopenhauer, Kant, and Compassion*, Kantian
     Review, Vol. 17, No. 3 (November, 2012), p. 403.
114) Ibid., p. 404.
115) Ibid., p. 412.
116) Irwin Terence. *The Development of Ethics* Vol. III, New York:
     Oxford University Press, 2007, p. 264.

ANNOTATIONS & BIBLIOGRAPHY 207

117) Ibid., p. 269.
118) Ibid., p. 284.

Chapter 5

119) http://www.dictionary.com/browse/community.
120) Marx, Karl. *Capital* Vol I, tr. Ben Fowkes, London: Penguin Books, 1992, p. 2.
121) Ibid., p. 2.
122) Ibid., p. 3.
123) Ibid., p. 6.
124) Ibid., pp. 7-8.
125) Ibid., p. 35.
126) Ibid. p. 35.
127) http://www.dictionary.com/browse/sovereignty.
128) NIV Bible, Genesis 1:27.
129) Augustine of Hippo. *Confessions*, tr. Chadwick, H., Oxford: Oxford University Press, 1998. p. 3.
130) https://en.wikipedia.org/wiki/List_of_religious_populations
131) Marx, Karl. *Introduction to A Contribution to the Critique of Hegel's Philosophy of Right*. Collected Works, v. 3. New York. 1976.
132) A traditional Korean saying from ancient times.
133) Socrates quoted by Plato in: *Republic*, 354b-c (conclusion of book I)
134) *Merriam-Webster's Encyclopaedia of World Religions*, ed. Wendy Doniger. Springfield: Merriam-Webster, 1999. p.709.
135) Pogge, Thomas. *World Poverty and Human Rights*, Malden: Polity Press, 2008, pp. 58-59.
136) Ibid., p. 63.
137) Ibid., p. 64.
138) Ibid., p. 70.
139) Ibid., p. 71.
140) The African Philosophy Reader, ed. P.H.Coetzee, A.P.Z. Roux, Wiredu, Kwasi. *Morality in African Thought*, London: Routledge, 2003. p. 377.
141) Journal of Buddhist Ethics Vol.2, Mar. 1995, Keown, Damien. *Are There "Human Rights" in Buddhism?*, p. 14.
142) Ibid., p. 15.
143) Ibid., p. 16.
144) Ibid., p. 21.
145) Cranston, Maurice W. What are *Human Rights?* London: Bodley Head, 1973, p. 43.
146) Abraham Lincoln. *Gettysburg Address*, Nov. 19, 1863.
147) A famous Korean saying from around 15 century.
148) From birth to death, throughout life, as in This health plan will

cover you from cradle to grave. Richard Steele used the term in The Tatler (1709): "A modest fellow never has a doubt from his cradle to his grave."

BIBLIOGRAPHY

Kant, Immanuel. *Critique of Pure Reason*, tr. Guyer, Paul. and Wood, Allen W. New York: Cambridge University Press, 2008.

Hense, Elisabeth. & Maas Frans. ed. *Towards a Theory of Spirituality*, Walpole: Peeters, 2011.

Russell, Bertland. *A History of Western Philosophy*, New York: Simon and Schuster, 1946.

Plato. *The Dialogues of Plato*, tr. Jowett, B. New York: Boni & Liveright, 1927.

Aristotle. *On the Soul*, trans. Smith, J. A, New York: Random House, 1941.

Chandler, Storer. H. E. H., *The Historical Development of the Philosophical Concept of the Soul or the Spirit*, Thesis of ANTS, 1935.

Augustin of Hippo. *De Trinity*, Cambridge: Cambridge University Press, 1967.

Augustine of Hippo. *Confessions*, tr. Chadwick, H., Oxford: Oxford University Press, 1998.

Aquinas T. *Summa Theolgie*, New York: McGraw-Hill Book Company, 1964.

Trigg Roger. *Ideas of Human Nature*, Oxford: Basil Blackwell, 1988.

Descartes, Rene. *Discourse on Method and Meditations*, Indianapolis: Bobbs-Merrill Company, 1960.

Spinoza, Benedict. De, *Ethic*, London: Oxford University Press, 1927.

Berkeley, George. *Berkeley Essay, Principles, Dialogues*, ed. Calkins, W. M., New York: Charles Scribner's Sons, 1929.

Hume, David. *On Human Nature and Understanding*, New York: Collier Books, 1962.

Kant, Immanuel. *Kritik der reinen Vernunft*, Hamburg: Felix Meiner, 1956.

Hegel, G. W. F. *Phänomenologie des Gesites*, Hamburg: Felix Meiner, 1980.

Hegel, G. W. F. *Grundlinien der Philosophie des Rechts*, Hamburg: Felix Meiner, 1956.

Hegel, G. W. F. *Phenomenology of Spirit*, Oxford: Clarendon Press, 1977.
Han, Sang Y. *A Research on Horkeimer's Critique of Reason*, Seoul: Yonsei Unversity, 2005.
Horkheimer, Max. *Critical Theory*, tr. Matthew J., New York: Herder and Herder, 1972.
Back, Seung G. *Dialectic Critical Theory*, Seoul: Kyungmonsa, 1982.
Marcuse, Herbert. *Reason and Revolution*, tr. Kim, Hyun I., Seoul: Choongwonmunwhasa, 2008.
McCarthy, Thomas A. *The Critical Theory of Jürgen Habermas*, Cambridge: MIT Press, 1978.
Armstrong, David M. *A Materialist Theory of the Mind*, New York: Routeledge, 1968.
Paul, Thagard. "Cognitive Science". In *The Stanford Encyclopedia of Philosophy* (Fall 2008), ed. Zalta, Edward N. http://en.wikipedia.org/wiki/Cognitive_science.
Aalon, Sloman, "The Mind as a Control system," In *Philosophy and Cognitive Science*, ed. Hookway, C. & Peterson, D. (New York: Cambridge University Press, 1983).
Steggink, Otger. "Study in Spirituality in Retrospect." in *Studies in Spirituality* 1 (2006): 8.
Waaijman, Kees. "*Spirituality as Theology.*", in *Studies in Spirituality* 21 (2011): 1-43.
Kenny, Anthony. *The Anatomy of the Soul*, Bristol: Basic Blackwell, 1978.
Gelven, Michael. *Spirit and Existence*, Notre Dame: University of Notre Dame Press, 1990.
Frank, L. I. *Man's Soul*, Athens: Ohio University Press, 1994.
Marx, Karl, *The Critique of Gotha Program, Part I*, 1875
Cassirer, Earnest. *An Essay On Man*, New Haven: Yale University Press, 1976.
Nietzsche, Friedlich. *Thus Spoke Zarathustra*, tr. R.Z. Hollingdale, London:
  Penguin Classics Edition, 1969.
Sartre, Jean P. *Existentialism Is a Humanism*, New Haven: Yale University Press, 2007.

Camus, Albert. *Second Letter to a German Friend*, December 1943.
Kant, Immanuel. *Groundwork for the Metaphysics of Morals*, trans. Thomas K. Abbott, Ontario: Broadview Press, 2005.
Schopenhauer, Arthur. *On the Basis of Morality*, trans. E. F. J. Payne, Indianapolis: Hackett Publishing Company, 1995.
Tsanoff, Radoslave A. *Schopenhauer's Criticism of Kant's Theory of Ethics, The Philosophical Review*, Vol. 19, No. 5 (Sep., 1910)
Guyer, Paul. *Schopenhauer, Kant, and Compassion*, Kantian Review, Vol. 17, No. 3 (November, 2012), p. 403.
Irwin, Terence. *The Development of Ethics* Vol. III, New York: Oxford University Press, 2007
Marx, Karl. 1976. *Introduction to A Contribution to the Critique of Hegel's Philosophy of Right*. Collected Works, v. 3. New York.
Lincoln, Abraham. *Gettysburg Address*, Nov. 19, 1863.
The Holy Bible. *New International Version*, Grand Rapids: Zondervan, 1978.
Aristotle. *Nicomachean Ethics*, tr. Irwin T. Indianapolis: Hackett Publishing Company, 1999.
Marx, Karl. *Capital* Vol I, tr. Ben Fowkes, London: Penguin Books, 1992
Heidegger, Martin. *Being and Time,* tr. Stambaugh, Joan, Albany: SUNY, 2010.
Lama, Dalai. *Buddhism: One Teacher, Many Traditions,* Somerville: Wisdom Publication, 2014.
Seo, Kyung D. *On Ghost's Life and Death*, Seoul: Dongwha Publishing Company, 1974.
Lim, Hyung S. *Reading of I Ching,* Seoul: Sechang Publishing Company, 2017.
Lyoo, Seung G. *History of Korean Confucianism*, Seoul: Sungkyunkwan Univ. Press, 2008.
Smith, Huston. *The World's Religions*, New York: HarperCollins Publishers, 1991.
Laozi. *Tao Te Ching*, tr. Park, Il B. Seoul: Yookmunsa, 2011.
Zhuang Zhou. Zhuangzi, tr. Oh Kang N. Seoul: Hyunamsa, 1999.
Guthrie, William K. *The Greek Philosophers: From Thales to Aristotle*, New York: Harper & Low Publishers, 1975.
McKeon, Richard. *Selections from Medieval Philosophers (Vol. 2)*, New

York: SophiaOmni Publishing, 2015.
Lindley, David. *Uncertainty: Einstein, Heisenberg, Bohr, and the Struggle for the Soul of Science,* New York: Landom House, 2007.
Hawking, Stephen. *A Brief History of Time,* New York: Bantam Books, 1996.
Kant, Immanuel. *Critique of Practical Reason,* tr. Pluhar, Werner S. Indianapolis: Hackett Publishing Company, 2009.
Pogge, Thomas. *World Poverty and Human Rights,* Malden: Polity Press, 2008.
The African Philosophy Reader, ed. P.H.Coetzee, A.P.Z. Roux, Wiredu, Kwasi. *Morality in African Thought,* London: Routledge, 2003.
Journal of Buddhist Ethics Vol.2, Mar. 1995, Keown, Damien. *Are There "Human Rights" in Buddhism?*
Cranston, Maurice W. What are *Human Rights?* London: Bodley Head, 1973.
http://en.wikipedia.org/wiki/Rational_animal.

http://www.dictionary.com/browse/community.
http://www.dictionary.com/browse/sovereignty.
https://en.wikipedia.org/wiki/List_of_religious_populations.

ANNOTATIONS & BIBLIOGRAPHY

◆ ABOUT THE AUTHOR

Rev. Sang Yun Han (James Han)

-BA (University of Massachusetts Boston, Philosophy, Summa Cum Laude)
-BA (Excelsior College, Literature in English, Political Science)
-MA (Yonsei Univ. Graduate School, Philosophy)
-MDiv (Gordon Conwell Theological Seminary, Divinity)
-PhD (SungKyunKwan Univ. Graduate School, Philosophy)
o Senior Pastor, Boston International Church, Boston, MA, USA
o Korea Unification Activist, Novelist, Thinker, Preacher & Evangelist, English Educator